"There is an abundance of management books on the market today, all of which provide some great information about managing people. The big challenge that I have found in reading those books is that they share how to manage people. People don't want to be 'managed.' They want to be 'led.' Enter David Long's book, "Built To Lead"...

The straightforward approach David takes is a breath of fresh air in this over-fluffed market of management books. I have spent thousands of dollars on consultants, and been in companies that have spent tens of thousands of dollars, all of which produced very minimal results. The ideas, techniques, and "step by step" approach David takes will drive your managers to a new level, and in turn will drive everyone they touch to new heights as well. You now have in your hands the MOST COMPLETE training course, seminar, and management consultant combined within the glossy covers of this book. My only hope for you is that this book becomes your #1 Go-To Guide, and doesn't just sit on your shelf and collect dust!"

—Dan Deigan,
www.LittleConversationsToday.com

"Just because you attain a position of authority doesn't make you a leader. Effective leadership requires going above and beyond being a 'boss.' In "Built To Lead," David Long teaches the skills and mindset necessary to become a Top 10% Manager. This is a book you will want to come back to again and again."

—Josh Hinds
Author and founder of www.GetMotivation.com

"David Long is 'the' expert for go-to leadership lessons, tools and advice to apply right away and shift your success to extremely heightened levels. He stands out as someone who truly wants others to soar and move forward fearlessly, and it shows in his tips, stories and examples throughout this excellent book."

—Kim Somers Egelsee
#1 best selling author of Getting Your Life to a Ten +

"David truly understands what it takes to manage people. His company is a shining example of how far engaged employees can take an organization. I am continually impressed at how motivated and excited his employees are when I speak to them, and I have implemented several of his ideas with my own staff. I (and my employees) are very grateful for the culture we enjoy in our firm, and we owe a great deal to David's teachings."

—Rob Rickert, CPA

As a prudent businessman, and a friend, I would say that anyone would be wise to listen to the advice that David gives on life lessons he has learned, from both business successes and failures and how to live a good, honest life. His friendship has made an impact on me and I always value the time I get to spend with him and his wife because he makes me better for it. The Bible says, "Iron sharpens iron" and the wounds of a friend are faithful. I will always be proud to call him my friend and mentor, and all those who read his book will be able to call him the same."

—Bill Willetts
Regional Sales Manager, Commercial & Industrial
Snap-on Tools

"I have read several books on management of people and the process in business, but in "Built to Lead - 7 Management R.E.W.A.R.D.S. Principles for Becoming a Top 10% Manager" Dave has so clearly outlined and detailed the path to success. The key ingredient here is YOU! Will YOU make the commitment to learn, grow and better yourself in order to lead your people more effectively? Dave lives the examples he gives, and has the proven, successful experience to show you how to truly change your understanding and relationship with your employees. Those managers who choose to read this book and invest in themselves will be challenged to immediately improve systems, change their own behavior and expect more and better from their team."

—Jon Carne, Port City Apparel www.portcityapparel.com

"You sure know how to write a GREAT BOOK! You definitely penetrated the bull's-eye with this one."

—Tony Johnson
2 Dream Productions, Inc.

"Leadership talk is cheap and plentiful. But spend some time with David Long and his wise and entertaining stories, and you will make a quantum leap in how your team responds to you! Read this book!"

—Dr. Barbara Weaver Smith,
Founder and CEO - The Whale Hunters, Inc.
www.TheWhaleHunters.com

"Built To Lead" sets a whole new standard for companies who want to stand out above the rest. In the financial world those who aren't built to lead get left behind. I was given David Long's book as a must read from one of my clients. I must admit with my busy schedule I don't get to read much more than industry-related materials, but after reading "Built To Lead" I have a whole new predilection for business books. Investing in yourself and in your people are always a sure bet for internal growth and your bottom line. You will find your ROI will bring you lifetime dividends.

—Thom Newcomb
MBA, CRPC Private Wealth Manager

"Just wanted to let you know that I finally got to read your book. To be honest with you, the last three chapters gripped me, so I re-read the entire book. Now, that is a compliment! I normally read 3-4 books per week, and do not often (as in rarely, nearly never) re-read any of them.

After reading your book, it struck me in a unique way. It is a book that contains seven principles that individually impact success. However, they cannot be easily separated. In fact, their greatest impact will be felt if they are embraced together as a whole and as a 'life-strategy.'

My suggestion is that a person sit down and read this book as a whole, handling it in its first sitting as a story. Upon completion, return to it with paper and pen and re-read it as a manual. When read as a story, the book is a fast paced, interactive conversation with a man who is sharing his heart with the reader. This book is an in-depth dialogue with many of the greatest management resources ever written, catalogued in a principled way so that they are a ready resource for anyone who wants to pursue management success.

The most striking thing about the book is that it leaves you with the profound sense that true management success is not about finding ways to make yourself successful, but in realizing that you will be successful if you find ways to make others successful. David: This should be no surprise to me, since, through our friendship, I have come to discover that is exactly what you have spent your life doing."

—Pastor Alan Benson
Bethel Baptist Church
Schaumburg, IL

I have owned and run businesses since I was 19 years old. I built my business fast but never learned how to manage the business or the people. There was a season when I went through new employees every week. I wish I had read David's book back then. This book was the missing piece of the puzzle. It's taught me where I went wrong and how I can properly manage my employees, which will lead to the growth of my business. The book is practical and very well written. I wrote so many notes I could write a sequel to the book. I highly recommend this book to become the manager you need to be to create success!

— Kimanzi Constable
Best-selling author, International speaker, Huffington Post
contributor

BUILT TO LEAD

Built to Lead – David Long

BUILT TO LEAD

7 MANAGEMENT R.E.W.A.R.D.S.
PRINCIPLES FOR BECOMING A
TOP 10% MANAGER

DAVID LONG

NEXT CENTURY
PUBLISHING

Built to Lead—7 Management R.E.W.A.R.D.S. Principles for Becoming a Top 10% Manager

Published in the United States of America by Next Century Publishing

www.NextCenturyPublishing.com

ISBN: 978-162-903-0463

Copy/Final Editor: Elisabeth Boehm and Simon Presland
Pre-proof Editor: Larry Smith
Cover Design: Adi Bustaman

Version 1.0 – www.Top10Manager.com/updates

Build yourself. Build your team.
And, together, you will be...
Built to Lead.

Dedication

First of all, I want to thank The Lord for blessing me, as Financial Guru Dave Ramsey says, "Far more than I deserve." The mistakes I've made in my life (and they are many) have all made me who I am today.

Many times I could not see the upside of tough times until I was on the mountain top, and could objectively look back down into the "valley of despair" I had emerged from, and say, "Thank you, God, for knowing exactly what I needed in my life." He always does.

I have story after story of how I was so certain something happening in my life was an utter disaster, and then it would turn into a complete triumph I could never have imagined. But alas, that would require me to write another book, so we'll wait to hear those stories another day.

Second, I want to thank my beautiful wife, Janet, for staying beside me through good times and bad. My life would definitely not be as fulfilled and happy if she was not at my side. She is what's best about me.

I want to thank my children for their love and support through the years, and for giving Janet and me five beautiful grandchildren.

Thank you, Mom and Dad, for teaching me right from wrong, and instilling in me (and my five siblings) a love for God.

Last, I want to thank my wonderful employees, both past and present, for being a huge part of my success as a business leader. The ride has been rough at times, but we persevered, and now we are reaching heights we never dreamed of. As of this writing, we are in the top 1% in our industry, and I owe a great deal of that success to my "troops."

I love all of you! My family, friends, and employees. You all make me rush to get out of bed each day! I love what I do, and it's largely because of who I get to do it with each day. Thank you all so much for that.

How to Get the Most from this Book

Read through the entire book to get a feeling and basic understanding of the magnitude and strength of the strategies (principles, if you will). In order to get the maximum benefit from what you learn in the book, I would have a highlighter in hand (for the printed version), or make good use of the "highlight" function within the Kindle version.

Once you've gone completely through the book, and have highlighted the most memorable parts that resonate with you, immediately go back to the beginning and read ONLY the highlighted portions again. This has been proven to greatly enhance your retention.

Once you've finished the highlighted portions, immediately go to your smart phone and create a reminder, one month into the future. This will remind you to reread the highlighted portions again. PLUS, it will help you remember that you haven't implemented all the principles you intended to act on. I would then add a reminder for repeating this process every six months. Remember, doing one push-up does not make a body fit and healthy. Repetition is the key to success in anything.

Tony Robbins said, "Success leaves clues." This reading strategy I've just shared with you will greatly help you to RETAIN what you read, and will exponentially increase your final results.

I would be honored if you would SHARE parts of the book (on Facebook and Twitter) that you find beneficial, and believe could help others. I would be very grateful if you would spread the word about the book.

BUILT TO LEAD

Table of Contents

Foreword

Many people talk about leading by example, but only a few actually do it. Over the past fifteen years I have worked directly with dozens of CEOs and their leadership teams, and have rarely encountered a culture of people who are as efficient, effective, and engaged as David Long's employees... This is extremely rare!

Rare, but not surprising, considering that I have seen up close why David's employees love, respect, and trust him. He constantly demonstrates his appreciation for commitment and performance that raises the bar of excellence in the company, and he has taught his management team to do the same.

David is fiercely committed to his employees' continued learning. He hosts Book Clubs (which he'll tell you about), buying books and freeing time each week for groups of employees to discuss what they've read. These aren't just books about how to do your job better; they are practical, inspiring books about how to live a good life – how to be financially solid, how to get along with people, how to be constantly improving your attitude and skills in all areas.

Don't think that David is a micro-manager. He places full trust in his key employees and actually takes a lot of time off – another rare accomplishment for a founder/owner! His company has excellent processes and procedures in place and a powerful collaborative team, so things run well without his looking over everyone's shoulder.

But a lot of leaders who are warm and caring about employees and make the workplace highly enjoyable do not make the hard decisions about people who don't pull their weight, thereby undermining the loyalty of everyone else. Not David. He gives everyone a fair opportunity, provides plenty of training and encouragement, and expects nothing less than your best effort. But anyone who fails to produce and to grow in their capabilities is quickly shown the door.

So I'm extremely glad he's written this book about his leadership principles and practices, with lots of advice for you about how to improve your company's performance by creating a workplace of fully engaged employees. Leadership talk is cheap and plentiful. But spend some time with David Long and his wise and entertaining stories and you will make a quantum leap in how your team responds to you!

Dr. Barbara Weaver Smith
Founder and CEO
The Whale Hunters, Inc.

Introduction

Do you remember the scene from the movie Moonstruck where Cher rushes over, gets in Nicolas Cage's face, slaps him upside the head a few times, and yells, "Snap out of it!"? Yeah, me too. That was definitely the most memorable moment in the film.

There's a YouTube link on our website that will take you directly to the scene I'm talking about. Go to: www.Top10Manager.com/Slap.

Why would I bother mentioning that movie scene to you?

Because, during the course of reading my book, it's vitally important that I, figuratively speaking...

Grab you by the lapels,
Pull you up close to my face,
> **Slap you upside the head a couple of times,**
>> **And scream into your face... "Snap out of it!**

This is your Management Career we're talking about here!"

Oh, and by the time we're done, my plan is to have you THANK ME for smacking you upside the head too!

That's how confident I am that what I have to share with you will help you become a much more successful manager and business leader.

That's right! I know beyond a shadow of a doubt that this book will teach you several new *best practices* that you've never learned or possibly never heard of before. **In fact, if I fail to teach you some new insight that will help you be more successful as**

a manager, you won't have to pay for my book. Yes, I know that's unheard of in the publishing world, but that is my guarantee to you.

You shouldn't have to pay for something if you don't benefit from it, right?

Of course not!

All I ask is that you be completely honest with me (as I'm being with you), and read the book cover to cover, and implement all of my management success strategies within the first two months.

Then, after six months, take an inventory of the successes you've experienced (and the lives you've helped change) thus far. If, at that time, you believe I have failed to deliver on my promises, feel free to ask me for your money back.

It's really that simple. You and I are starting a relationship that I believe will last for many years, so the last thing I want to do is be perceived as someone who did not deliver on his promises to you.

Our mission here is to help you become a Top 10% Manager in your company, or industry. I'm not interested in mere incremental gains making you an extra few thousand dollars more a year. Oh, please! That's peanuts, and you're better than that! Seriously! You can earn that much by buying a lawn mower and cutting your neighbor's yards every weekend, or babysitting the neighbor's bratty kids. No thanks. That was fine when you were a teenager, but not today! I'm talking about a "life changing" increase in your income. I'm talking about the kind of money that sets you apart and makes your peers, friends, and family members sit up and take notice.

Plain and simple, we're going to learn critical instruction you were NOT taught in your company's Management Training Program on how to be successful. Knowing how to read profit and loss statements is one thing, and that's definitely important, but it's not going to take you to the next level. What I'm going to share with you will. We're going to create a career for you that will have you looking back with pride, and saying, "Look at the career success I was able to accomplish. But, more importantly, look at the impact I have had on the lives of hundreds (or maybe thousands) of my employees and their families. That is my finest accomplishment."

After learning and implementing the things I will teach you, you should expect to double your income in the next three years, if not sooner!

That's not me "blowing smoke" either. Later, I will share with you several stories of people whose lives I've been fortunate enough to touch through the years. I'll allow them to share with you, in their own words, how I've helped them greatly improve their lives and incomes. Oh, and some have more than tripled, or quadrupled, their incomes in only a few years. Yes, it can be done.

Ok, so let's get started on our journey together!

Chapter 1

If YOU fail as a Manager... here are 3 Reasons WHY it will happen.

*"Of all sad words of mouth or pen,
the saddest are these: 'it might have been.'"*
—John Greenleaf Whittier

"Houston, we have a problem!" Tom Hanks frantically exclaimed in the 1995 movie, *Apollo 13*, as he restated the famous words of Astronaut Jack Swigert during the ill-fated Apollo 13 mission to the moon. Though your "problem" might not actually be life-threatening, statistically speaking, you've probably got some real issues as a manager RIGHT NOW that could most definitely kill your career.

It's been my experience that most managers are clueless they have a serious problem until the owner, district manager, or another member of upper management, shows up and says, "I need your keys." By that time, it's too late for me to help you.

I'm sure you would prefer not to receive one of those unannounced, and very unpleasant key visits, so let's make sure you don't. From this day forward, and while you still have time, we're going to help you take control of your own career success and create your own future.

Let's take a moment to look at the "problem" with a few statistics on the failure rate of managers today. This is what you're up against:

According to the 2010 *World at Work Research Report*, the average percentage of the employee population that was promoted to management during 2009 (the last fiscal year's data) was a mere 7%. (Note: This 7% seems to be a consistent trend/average over many years, and it includes ALL promotions, including additional career moves beyond the first management position.)

So basically, for every 100 employees hired, only six or seven will be promoted to their first management position. If you're a manager now, and you probably are if you're reading this book, "Congratulations!" You're one of the 7% who made it!

That's the good news.

Now, here's the bad news.

Statistically speaking, you won't be promoted again. The vast majority of these first time managers will eventually fail. Only one in seven will stay in management with their present company.

The rest? One or two of them may possibly be moved laterally, giving them another opportunity in another city. But, most likely, they'll eventually be canned.

To illustrate this point, take a moment and think about how many of your manager friends are no longer employed by your company, and you'll begin to see how accurate these statistics are.

Our goal, with both of us working together, is to make sure you're the ONE (out of those seven formerly promoted managers) who makes it to the next level. Alright, so: **What is the NUMBER ONE REASON managers fail?**

They go to the office every day... but they don't really LEAD.

Years ago, I read the *The E-Myth*, a book written by the highly acclaimed management guru, Michael Gerber.

According to Gerber, the number one problem for managers today is, "They're so busy working IN their business... they NEVER WORK ON IT!"

In other words, if you, as the manager, merely show up every day, make sure everyone is doing their jobs, and go home, you've totally missed what your main responsibility is – strategically systemizing and growing the business through effective leadership. That's the KEY!

But how do you make that happen? That's the thing I really like about Gerber. He helped me understand the need for creating duplicable and documented processes in the correct, *absolute best way to do each job* within the business. This will *save your team massive amounts of wasted time and frustration.* Having documented processes clarifies each responsibility and makes it easy to train new employees. That's how you successfully lay the foundation for massive growth.

If you never do anything beyond the mundane and ordinary to improve the company's future results, the end result for YOU will be a significantly shortened management career.

Whether your strategy is to do as little as possible and whine about the results, or to do as much as possible, only work on the minute tasks required to run your company, you're headed for complete failure.

One of my good friends, **Kyle Wilson (www.KyleWilson.com /52Lessons)**, also read Gerber's book. Kyle provides a great description of why your effort to make sure your business is running smoothly isn't good enough by itself.

Here's what Kyle shared with me...

(Note: every time Kyle mentions "founder" or "owner," substitute the word "manager," because the same can be said of us.)

The premise of Michael's book is that most small businesses get started and are run by a Technician, an Entrepreneur, or a Manager. And, according to Gerber, the #1 reason most small businesses don't succeed long-term is because they are started by a Technician.

A Technician is someone who knows how to do the technical work involved in a job, without much thought to the two other equally important roles, the Entrepreneur and the Manager. Now, a technician, in this case, is someone who is an expert in his or her particular field. For example: You are a great cook, so all your friends say you should open a restaurant. Or, maybe you love decorating, so you start an interior design business.

Now, here is where the light really came on for me. Michael lays out the importance of making sure, no matter how big or small your business is, you write out (in great detail) all the different roles needed for the continued success of your company. You then create long-term, sustainable "systems" (much like a franchise) to support each of these supporting roles.

He states that if the business is to thrive, it must move beyond the founder. A business wholly dependent on the founder and their abilities is not really a business, but rather a very burdensome job for the founder. Every time you are out sick or take a vacation or are otherwise absent, the business stops as well.

It's so easy in the beginning of a business to hire people and just delegate all the areas you perceive as "not your thing" versus identifying upfront all the needed roles and building a plan where you, as the CEO, strategically create the right systems and train people into those positions. Sometimes you have to do it wrong to be totally teachable and open to doing it right."

There's a link to Gerber's book on our website at www.Top10Manager.com/Resources, if you're interested.

Personally, I would buy the audio version too, so you can listen to it (over and over again to really learn the information) while driving to/from work. That's a far better use of your time than listening to the radio, and doing so will pay off, I assure you.

I don't think you are the type of manager who is only concerned with punching the time clock. You wouldn't be reading this book right now if you were. You've taken the first step to greatly improve your chances of success as a manager. You've already "planted the seeds" of success by taking action. Now let's continue, and make those seeds GROW!

As we've learned, the first reason that managers fail is because they spend too much time working *in* their business instead of *on* it.

What is the NUMBER TWO REASON managers fail?

Their employees don't genuinely believe managers CARE about them.

Because we are human and inherently selfish, we all constantly ask ourselves, "What's in it for me?" As a result, we rarely care as much about our people as we should.

So, beyond the obvious fact that it would be selfish, why should you care about the success of your people, and not just your own success?

Allow me to illustrate this with a real-world example.

Have you ever visited Amish Country in Pennsylvania? I have, and it's beautiful country. The Amish are all about "community." Many times they'll come together as a group to help build a barn (maybe to replace one that has burned down), or perhaps to build a house for a recently married couple.

If you've never witnessed the process of how they complete a barn raising, then you can see them do it in the movie *Witness*, released back in the mid-80s, starring Harrison Ford.

There's a clip showing what I'm talking on our Resources page at www.Top10Manager.com/Resources. Just look for *Barn Raising*.

Check it out, and you'll see everyone working together to get the job done.

As you watch the video, notice how everyone is scurrying around hammering wooden pins or lifting timbers into place. Everything is done by a team of people on a mission to complete the task together in the most efficient manner. You'll notice that everyone seems happy during this process too. That's the way it should be.

And then, if you drive further down the road, you might see one guy trying to build a barn on his own.

Correct me if I'm wrong, but I doubt we would see any smile on his face!

Hmmm... imagine how long it will take him to build the barn all by himself. Is it even possible? Will he break his back trying to lift those heavy beams into place? Will he succeed, or will he become frustrated and quit? My money says, "He'll quit when he realizes how hard it is to build his barn all by himself!"

Admit it: It's a pretty pathetic way to try to build anything, especially a business.

Yet, this is exactly what the average manager tries to do. They think they can "herd their unruly cats" into doing their bidding through their sheer force of will (and threats). Or, maybe as I've heard some managers foolishly say, "Because I pay them to!"

Bad move, Sparky.

For some reason, I suddenly think of young Oliver Twist in the English orphanage, holding up his empty bowl and saying, "Please, sir, I want some more!"

If you exhibit, by your attitude, that you view yourself as the "almighty lord of the business" and your employees as "privileged peasants," you, my friend, are headed for the "exit door" of your management career.

Why?

Well, obviously, this attitude results in a manager-versus-employees mentality. In this hostile environment, employee loyalty and commitment to you, their boss, will not exist. You might be successful getting your people to work harder, longer, and faster by your sheer force of will... but that will only work in the short run. In the long run, you will ultimately fail.

These poor saps, and I sincerely hope you're not one of them, never understand WHY their management career comes to an end. It's because they never understood, nor fully grasped, the concept of effectively using leverage.

Now, some people will misconstrue what I'm about to tell you, wrongly labeling it as manipulation. But, allow me to tell you the difference. **Manipulation**, as defined by the dictionary, means "**to**

control or play upon by artful, unfair, or insidious means especially to one's own advantage."

Motivation, on the other hand, means "providing a reason for someone to act a certain way."

If you continuously threaten your employees with phrases like, "If you do that again, I'm going to cut your hours" or you embarrass an employee in front of their peers by belittling how they did a particular task, you're trying to **manipulate** them. This is clearly selfish and wrong.

But, if you encourage your employees by praising their work and providing ways for them to improve their lives (in virtually every way, not only in ways specifically related to their jobs) through what they call "educational opportunities," you are trying to **motivate** them. The beauty of using motivation: you don't need to use a cattle prod to get engaged employees to work, and work hard!

That describes the difference between the two methods of getting your employees to perform at a higher level within your business. As a manager, you need this mindset to be understood, implemented, and adopted by every member of the team in order to become successful together! EVERYONE wins, and that's our goal.

I'm not sure where I read this, but it further exemplifies what I'm talking about.

> *"Success... is Making a Difference in the Lives of Others.*
> *Happiness... is Watching them Grow Because of It."*

One of the greatest lessons I've learned in my 56 years of life is summarized in a quote from one of my many mentors (though we never met). Here's the only true path to management success:

> *"You can have everything you want in life*
> *IF you will just help others get what they want!"*
> —Zig Ziglar, the late (and great) motivational speaker

Do you fully understand the meaning of that statement? It's extremely powerful. Please don't just skim over it. If I were you, I would read it again and again, until you fully grasp the fact that you'll never be successful until you make sure others are successful FIRST. We're talking about your employees, but the same thing can also be said for your clients or customers.

If they're not happy, they will go somewhere else, and you would do the same thing. Constantly losing and then replacing employees (and customers) will never make you successful. In fact, it will get you fired.

Andrew Carnegie, the Great American Industrialist, said this:

> *"No man will make a great leader who wants to do it all himself*
> *or get all the credit for doing it."*

It's amazing what a team of engaged, motivated employees can accomplish when no one is seeking to get the credit for the success. Since building a business is a team effort, everyone should get credit for its success. Remember, "No man is an island."

One of my favorite books is **Dale Carnegie's, *How to Win Friends and Influence People***. Here's an excerpt from that book to illustrate this point about motivation and the power it wields:

> Why did Andrew Carnegie pay Charles Schwab a million dollars a year or more than three thousand dollars a day? Why?
>
> Because Schwab is a genius?

No.

Because he knew more about the manufacture of steel than other people?

Nonsense.

Charles Schwab told me himself that he had many men working for him who knew more about the manufacture of steel than he did. Schwab says that he was paid this salary largely because of his ability to deal with people. I asked him how he did it.

Here is his secret, set down in his own words—words that ought to be cast in bronze and hung in every home and school, every shop and office in the land—words that children ought to memorize instead of wasting their time memorizing the conjugation of Latin verbs or the amount of the annual rainfall in Brazil—words that will all but transform your life and mine if we will only live them: "I consider my ability to arouse enthusiasm among the men," said Schwab, "the greatest asset I possess, and the way to develop the best that is in a man is by appreciation and encouragement. There is nothing else that so kills the ambitions of a man as criticisms from his superiors. I never criticize anyone. I believe in giving a man incentive to work. So I am anxious to praise but loath to find fault. If I like anything, I am hearty in my approbation and lavish in my praise."

That is what Schwab did. But what does the average manager do? The exact opposite. If he doesn't like a thing, he raises the Old Harry; if he does like it, he says nothing. "In my wide association in life, meeting with many and great men in various parts of the world," Schwab declared, "I have yet to find the man, however great or exalted his station, who did not do better work and put forth greater effort under a spirit of approval than he would ever do under a spirit of criticism."

When you are "lavish in your praise," as Schwab stated, there is no end to your potential success. There's no end in how much your employees will do for you.

As a result of the lack of praise coming from the average manager, employee engagement and loyalty have never been as low as they are today.

Here's a quote from a recent article written for Forbes Magazine by Dov Seidman. *"For years, employee engagement scores have declined despite the millions of dollars companies invest to boost sagging workforce morale. Engagement experts and practitioners continue to make commendable and reasoned efforts to encourage companies to better focus on and improve their engagement."*

Yes, the research is troubling for managers everywhere, but we're going to do our part to help fix that problem in your business.

OK, Dave, so what is the NUMBER THREE REASON managers fail?

They simply stop learning.

Regardless of whether an aspiring individual has earned a college degree or just barely finished high school... if he thinks he's done learning, he is foolish. Even if someone has earned a management position, there are no guarantees he'll keep it. In fact, statistically speaking, he won't.

Wherever you are in your education process, you are just getting started in what you need to learn in order to become a successful manager.

If you're wise you'll remember this quote:

"Not all readers are leaders, but ALL Leaders are Readers."
—President Harry S. Truman

If you're going to be an effective leader, you simply have to stay up to date on your knowledge within your industry and the coming trends of the future.

Bought a buggy whip lately? Yeah, me neither. Why? Because we have cars now, and very few people are still riding around in horse-drawn carriages. There were hundreds of buggy whip manufacturers in the nineteenth century, and there's only a handful now. Why? Because times change, and people and businesses need to change as well.

Here's a little secret: reading for knowledge has made me millions of dollars down through the years. Yes, millions.

As an example, here's just one idea I received from something I wasn't even supposed to see!

A little over 13 years ago, a magazine on manufacturing came across my desk purely by accident. I say "accident" because it was addressed to a business that had recently gone under in our office park, and somehow ended up in my mail. Like you, my first impulse was to throw it in the trash, but something stopped me. You might call it "luck," but I call it "Divine Providence."

I started thumbing through the pages, and I came across an article about *Kaizen*, the Japanese word for "continuous improvement." I'd never heard the term before, but through the course of reading the article I learned about W. Edward Deming, and how he revolutionized manufacturing in America. OK, so it wasn't really in America. It should have been America, but it was actually in Japan. Why Japan?

Because American manufacturers weren't interested in hearing what Deming had to say. They were immensely arrogant. They thought they knew it all and basically blew him off when he tried to share his research on how to improve their manufacturing processes, quality control standards, and greatly reduce waste in the process.

The main reason we know about Kaizen, or Lean Manufacturing as we call it in America today, is largely because of Mr. Deming. So, how did that happen if American manufacturers rejected Deming's help?

After the defeat of Japan in WWII, General Douglas MacArthur, the Allied Commander, was placed in charge of helping to rebuild Japan's completely destroyed economy. In an effort to understand exactly "who, what, when, and where" had to be done, Deming was brought over by the US Army to help with the Japanese census. But that is not where he would make his greatest impact.

If you're old enough to remember, it used to be that if a product said "Made in Japan" it meant you "weren't going to own it very long before it broke." Yeah, they were known for producing some pretty shoddy work back then.

But, here's the thing. They realized this, and had a passionate desire to learn new things and took action to improve their production methods.

After learning of Deming's expertise in quality control, the Japanese Union of Scientists and Engineers contacted Deming, and asked him if he would come help them. He graciously accepted, and as a result, and in large part to Deming's groundbreaking earlier work, the Japanese would later go on to create the now world famous Toyota Production System of Manufacturing.

"Wait, Dave! Isn't that the production system the Japanese manufacturers teach American businesses today?" Why, yes it is.

So, in large part, because of the arrogance of American business leaders in pre-WWII America (primarily in the automotive industry), the Japanese now teach Americans quality control methods.

Are you getting the idea of what I'm saying here? Good. I thought you might be.

As a business manager, and leader, are you as arrogant as the American manufacturers... or as hungry to learn and improve as the business leaders were in Japan after the war?

Here's a hint: Stay hungry to LEARN and IMPROVE!

Back to the magazine article...

By reading and adopting the mindset of constantly learning and improving myself and the company, I contacted the author of the article on Kaizen, and asked him a few questions. He graciously put me in touch with a Kaizen Consultant, and the rest is history. My team and I learned about the process known as a Kaizen Blitz, where a consultant comes in and does a mini-consulting project (two days, in this case) to point out the glaring mistakes in our manufacturing processes.

That started my quest to always look for the best way to do something, and that mindset permeates throughout our company today.

As a result, and largely because of always trying to learn new things, we are over 14 times more efficient than we were in early 2001. Like I said, "Millions..."

OK, so: FAILING TO LEAD, FAILING TO CARE, and FAILING TO LEARN are the top three reasons managers fail.

Now we're going to learn the 7 R.E.W.A.R.D.S. Principles that, if implemented, will catapult your career to the next level in record time. For the rest of the book, **I'm going to show YOU, step by step, through my "7 Management R.E.W.A.R.D.S. Success Principles," exactly how to become a world-class manager; one that will place you in the top 10% of managers in your company and industry**. And, as I've stated earlier, we're going to do it while greatly impacting and improving the lives of your employees—not just yours. My philosophy is truly a "win-win" for you AND the lives of everyone you touch every day.

But, before we do that, you may want to ask: "So, Dave, before I spend my time reading your book, what makes you think you're qualified to write about becoming a 'world class' manager?"

Good question! Let's find out.

Chapter 2

Got the Blood on my T-Shirt to prove it!

*"Our greatest weakness lies in giving up. The most
certain way to succeed is always to try just one
more time."*
—Thomas A. Edison

As they say, "I've been there, done that... and I definitely have the
blood on my T-shirt to prove it!"

If you ask just about anyone who has become successful in life,
they'll tell you it wasn't an easy path. More than likely, they dealt
with many failures and setbacks along the way... but they still
persisted. That's why so few make it to the top in their professions.
It's so much easier to quit.

As one who didn't quit, here's a little about me.

FIRST

I am the founder and CEO of one of the largest Employee
Engagement and Recognition companies on the planet. In fact, with
annual sales of $8,000,000, we're in the top 1% worldwide!

Our main company, MyEmployees (www.MyEmployees.com),
handles the employee engagement and recognition plaque programs
for approximately 12,000 active businesses in the US and Canada,

and has done so for the last 25 years.

We've worked with over 100,000 managers through those 25 years, and we've shown them how to effectively use their employee engagement and recognition programs to increase their sales, profits, employee loyalty and productivity, and their own personal success.

In fact, many of you reading this book are clients of ours. Allow me to let you know how much we appreciate you, and definitely want YOU, most of all, as our valued client, to benefit from what you'll learn here.

I've never shared this with you until now, although I've been asked to write this book for years. My goal is to help you, literally, "crush the competition," both within your company AND in your industry. Few managers will take the time to read this book, and I'm proud of you for being one of the few.

Anything less than your optimum success, and neither of us will be satisfied!

Let's continue...

Our company has also been blessed to be what is known in the business world as a "Gazelle."

You may be asking, "What the heck is a Gazelle, Dave?"

Here's the basic definition of a **Gazelle** from Investopedia, an online investment company:

"A high-growth company is one that is increasing its revenues by at least 20% annually for four years or more, starting from a revenue base of at least $1 million. This growth pace means that the company has effectively

doubled its revenues over a four-year period. As Gazelle companies are characterized by their rapid growth pace, rather than their absolute size, they can range in size from small companies to very large enterprises."

Actually, we've done it longer than four years, but hey, who's counting, right?

SECOND

The more important qualification to write this book, in my opinion, is the fact that...

I've been educated in the Real World.

Why does that matter? Well, even though I have a master's degree, any business person worth their salt will tell you...

> *"Your REAL EDUCATION doesn't even BEGIN... until you LEAVE SCHOOL!"*

I think Mark Twain said it best when he wrote,

"Don't let schooling interfere with your education."

Here's the deal. I don't care how many years of formal education you have if it doesn't add anything to your bank account, or more importantly, to your quality of life.

Former U.S. President Calvin Coolidge put it this way,

> *"Education will NOT make you successful;*
> *the world is FULL of Educated Derelicts."*

I don't know about you, but I've hired a few of these educated derelicts President Coolidge spoke of. They don't last very long around me. They seem to have the attitude of, "The world owes me a living because I've got this 'piece of paper'!" (They are referring to their diploma.)

News flash: "No it doesn't, bonehead!" Avoid these losers like the plague. They're a waste of your time. Let them be someone else's problem child. You'll just have to fire them later anyway, because they'll try to lord it over your other team members. As someone once said, "These people already think they're a legend... in their own mind." No thanks. I'll pass.

THIRD

Speaking of education, allow me share something embarrassing with you:

I can't begin to count how many mistakes I've made in my life.

Many years ago, I lost everything and had to move (along with my wife and three children) back in with my parents at age 31. As you can imagine, it was a rather humbling experience for me. Yes, ol' Dave here knows what it means to fail... and fail hard! But, there is a silver lining to that very dark cloud: I started my $8,000,000 business in my parent's garage. Maybe I'll share that story in my next book.

Here's another fact that I need to confess to you:

I've also lost/wasted well over $1,000,000 in my life.

Does that shock you? It shouldn't. I don't know any immensely successful people who have not experienced massive failure in their lifetimes.

But, here's the good news: thank the Good Lord I've made at least ten dollars for every one I've lost!

You'd probably agree, anyone who can get a 10:1 ratio of "wins to failures" is someone you can probably learn something from. I don't take that responsibility lightly.

I've accomplished something very rarely seen in business – or by any business leader anywhere, for that matter! I have become a Top 10% Manager in three separate, unrelated industries—Retail Management, Real Estate Investments, and the Employee Engagement and Recognition Industry—and have become a multimillionaire in the last two. Few businessmen can make that statement. I sincerely believe you can learn something from someone who has done that!

FOURTH

For many years, I have made it a habit to spend roughly three hours every day reading and learning ways to improve the prospects for success for our clients, our employees, and myself. The saying, "what got me here won't get me where I want to go," is true, so my quest for knowledge is unending. I have a personal library valued at over $300,000, and it's growing every day, literally.

Side note: Even though I have read countless books, listened to at least a gazillion audio books, perused innumerable research papers and articles on various subjects related to business... one thing stands out to me: (Note: This is the number one reason I've written this book.)

Very few management coaching materials bring it all together, showing how managers AND employees WIN TOGETHER. At least 90% of the management books focus on how you can improve, but never mention your people. That, to me, is a real problem. This book will teach you how to create a win for everyone, and that I have

guaranteed you.

Understanding that one of the secrets to my success is that I've read everything I could get my hands on pertaining to management and leadership, it's easy to see why I believe this:

> *"As long as you're green, you're growing.*
> *As soon as you're ripe, you start to rot."*
> —Ray Kroc, McDonald's Corporation

FIFTH

Darren Hardy, the Publisher of *Success Magazine*, recently held his first ever "**High Performance Forum**" in San Diego, CA, composed of successful entrepreneurs from around the world. I was fortunate to be chosen as one of only 24 business leaders in the inaugural group from over 3,000 applicants from all around the world.

SIXTH

Many years ago, in an effort to diversify our assets, I became a very successful real estate investor, and have millions of dollars in assets today with zero debt. In fact, the one remaining small property debt I did have (our 20,000 sq. ft. office building) was completely paid off recently.

SEVENTH

I have won innumerable awards in my life, including multiple "Salesman of the Month" awards (with different companies in different industries, including the mighty AT&T).

Out of a district of over 35 stores (in a national retail electronics chain), in three and a half years as a young manager in my late 20s, I won...

(14) "Manager of the Month" awards - two, "back to back" consecutive wins

(1) "Manager of the Year" award (in first place for eight straight months)

(1) "Runner-Up Manager of the Year" award

(3) Company earned trips to the Bahamas, Caribbean Cruise, and Switzerland

Here I am winning two "Manager of the Month" plaques from Joe, the best district manager I ever had. As the caption in the picture states, I won back-to-back monthly "Manager of the Month" plaques TWICE. Remember, this was with me competing against more than 35 other managers every month.

Double take

DM 0519 Joe Columbus (left) presents Dave Long with two recently earned Manager of the Month awards. The manager of Store 1907 in Rock Hill, S.C., produced the numbers necessary to win the January and February awards. This is the second year for Long to accomplish back-to-back awards. 1986

Like I said, I know what I'm talking about, and I have the track record to prove it. Beyond all that, and because of the success we've had in adding value to our clients' lives, Janet, my lovely wife of 35 years, and I have traveled extensively around the US, Canada, Mexico, the Caribbean, the Holy Land, and across Eastern Europe and the Mediterranean Sea.

If that's not enough for you, Janet and I have done something less than one in one million motorcycle riders have done. We both rode our Harley Davidson Road King Classic motorcycles on a six and a half week Sea to Shining Sea Tour (as Janet called our trip) from Wilmington, NC to San Francisco, CA in 2005. What a beautiful country we live in!

Understand this: my education and the principles I'm sharing with you in this book are not based on empty, pie-in-the-sky classroom theories spouted by professors who've never even run a lemonade stand, much less a multi-million dollar business! I wouldn't do that to you. Our company's success is tantamount to our helping you attain YOUR success as a manager!

If YOU fail, we fail.

When YOU win, we win.

That's all we desire for you and for ourselves.

Now that you know I'm qualified, let's get to the meat of this book.

Before we go any further, here's the question you need to answer for yourself: Do you REALLY want management success? Most people just say they do, while very few actively pursue success with a plan to achieve it. They fail to take any real, meaningful action to make it happen. You're not one of those people IF you finish this book, and implement what you learn here.

Tony Robbins said, "Success leaves clues!"
Oh, and by the way, so does failure.

You are where you are today because of the choices you've made throughout your lifetime... how you spend your time... both at work, and away from the office.

Did you know that the average American doesn't even read one book a year? How pathetic is that?!! Make sure you finish this one! Only then, can you benefit from my management success acronym featuring my...

7 Management R.E.W.A.R.D.S. Principles.

Ready to dive in?

Great! Let's go!

The first Principle of my

Management R.E.W.A.R.D.S. Principles.

(and represented by the first letter **R**) is...

Chapter 3

RECONNAISSANCE
(or "RECON" as it's called in the military)

Hire Right, Train, Prune, and Repeat!

WHERE are you Right NOW, and
WHAT should you do about it?

*"He who is prudent and lies in wait for an enemy
who is not, will be victorious."*
—Sun Tzu, *The Art of War*

During times of war, military commanders throughout history have sent out scouts to find the enemy. Why? Two reasons. First, knowledge of an enemy's whereabouts is key in achieving the "element of surprise," the single greatest advantage a commander can possess. Second, without knowledge of an enemy's location, the commander is blind and his unit is vulnerable to attack.

To secure the highest probability of victory, commanders must know the enemy's location at all times.

In the military, sending scouts to pinpoint an enemy's location is known as a "recon" mission.

I'm a bit of a military history nut, and one particular story that illustrates the importance of "recon" and "knowing where you stand in relation to your enemy" is the story of General Robert E. Lee in his second attempt to invade the northern states during America's Civil War.

Fresh from his victory at Chancellorsville, VA, General Lee felt it was time he "took the war to the north" in an effort to influence the northern politicians to sue for peace. As he neared Gettysburg, PA, Lee was unsure of the location of the northern troops, and what their strength (size of their armies) might be.

Having heard nothing from General Jeb Stuart, his most trusted Cavalry Commander and Chief Scout, Lee urgently sent out messengers.

According to The Battle of Gettysburg: A Guided Tour by Edward James Stackpole and Wilbur Sturtevant Nye, each messenger carried the same message. "General Stuart, where have you been? I have not heard a word from you for days and you are the 'eyes and ears' of my army."

Unbeknownst to Lee, Stuart and his cavalry forces were riding to the east, even though Lee had suggested that they go west. Lee believed that's where Stuart might find the elusive northern army. Despite the fact that Lee's recommendation to head west was not a direct order, he still assumed that was the direction Stuart went.

His assumption was wrong.

During the war, Stuart had been quite successful at finding and capturing wagon trains of badly needed supplies. With the soldiers in Lee's army surviving on minimal daily rations, you can be sure he was looking to do it again. As it so often happens with us, Stuart was distracted by "bright, shiny objects" and failed to stay focused on the most important part of the mission. Lee needed to know where the enemy was far more than he needed any amount of food Stuart and his men could possibly find. Last time I heard, dead soldiers don't need to eat!

Without this vital intelligence, Lee stumbled into the Battle of Gettysburg unaware and ill-prepared to face the enemy forces. The uncertainty he felt had an impact on his decision-making, the battle, and ultimately, the war. As we know now, this battle at Gettysburg was the turning point of the war.

The loss at Gettysburg was the greatest, single defeat the southern forces endured during the long, four years of conflict. It wasn't so much that they lost more men than the Union forces (as the numbers of losses were similar), as much as they didn't have as many to lose. Nearly a third of Lee's general officers were killed, wounded, or captured. The Confederate Army never fully recovered. The devastating lack of effective recon for this one single battle changed the outcome of the war.

Not knowing what forces he faced before him was the critical intelligence Lee needed to make the right decisions.

He never received it, and the result was the turning point of the war.

As you can see, it is extremely important for commanders to know, at all times, exactly where they are currently in relation to the forces they face.

That being said, the exact same principle can be applied to your management career and the situation you find yourself in today.

OK, so let's talk a little about your current situation. If you've not read

Jim Collins' great book, ***Good to Great***, you definitely should. If you don't have it, here's the link to purchasing his book:

http://www.amazon.com/dp/0066620996/

In his book, Jim asks an immensely critical question I will never forget. In fact, I try to ask myself this question every month or so, without fail. It's one of the most important questions you will ever ask yourself as a manager.

Jim asks, **"Do you have the right people on your bus?"** referring to the managers and employees you have on your team.

Having the right people on your team is the difference between extraordinary success... and utter failure. It's the difference between being an *average manager* for your entire career and being one who becomes a district manager, regional manager, or potentially even higher.

At our company, MyEmployees, we've known many client managers who were promoted to the next level in their careers. Probably the main reason we know about this is because, once they were promoted, they called us up and said, "I've been promoted! I want that same employee recognition program I used in my store for all 20 of the stores I have in my new district."

Now, where do you stand as the "bus driver" of your business? Are the right people on your bus? You need to determine that immediately!

First things first: **Think, specifically, about each member of your management team, and assess whether they should continue with you, or should they be replaced**. They're your "foundation," and they must be wholeheartedly supportive of your business goals, or you are guaranteed to fail. You simply cannot do it by yourself.

Next, you'll want to consider each employee that works for you. Should they continue as employees, be fired, or possibly be reassigned to another department within the company? Enlist the input of your top managers (and definitely their direct supervisors) to help make the most accurate decisions as to who stays and who goes.

Every successful general in the armed forces has to constantly monitor the make-up and competency of his forces. That responsibility, ultimately, falls to you.

Now, you've done your recon, identify any underperforming team members who have not improved after you (and your management team) have invested the necessary time and effort to help them improve.

I recently had a discussion with a management consultant about the characteristics of managers, and he plainly said to me, "There are some things you can fix, and some you cannot… regardless of how hard you try."

It reminds me of the old farmer who said, "You can take the pig out of the mud, but sooner or later, son, he'll go back… because that's his nature." You should do your very best to constantly train and improve your existing people to accomplish your goals, but some of them will need to be replaced. There's no company with perfect employees at every position.

What's next? You must take action.

I'll borrow from an idea put forth by **Brian Tracy**, another one of my many mentors, in his book *Change your Thinking, Change Your Life*:

"Knowing what you know now, and reviewing your life as it stands, is there anything that you would choose not to get involved

with if you had the choice to do it over again? Being able to abandon those things that no longer serve you well may in fact be one of the best ways to Change your Life!"

Ask yourself, **"Knowing what I know now about this individual, if I could go back in time, would I hire them again?"** If the answer is even close to being "no," then let them go today. *I mean now.* Today. Do not delay taking action, because if you do, you will not change the direction of your career.

Pardon me for saying so, but as hard as you try... and as much as you polish it... you're never going to turn a turd into a "brownie"!

So, stop trying to polish your turds! Throw them into someone else's yard, and move on!

Note: There are really only a few legitimate reasons you could have for not letting that person go today:

1: You fear your Corporate HR Department will "have a cow" and warn you not to let them go. This is really a problem today for larger companies, and I genuinely feel for them. But, let me ask you a question: Have you documented all the problems and communications you've had with this troublesome employee? If not, then you haven't done a very good job of protecting yourself and the company, and that's going to hurt your chances to get rid of the problem child employee.

Your next step is to enlist the help of the manager directly above you in helping you to talk to HR in your effort to get rid of them. Bottom line, you have an employee who is being disruptive, or a distraction at best, and a weight around your neck, and wrecking team moral at worst. They need to go. They are holding you hostage. If you've "covered your backside" (and the company's) like you should have, let them go.

Think long-term.

If the problem child employee is keeping your team from doing the best job it can possibly do, that person is costing the company money. Lots of it! Plus, if they are causing issues in your department, your good employees will become frustrated and leave you. Are the problem employees worth keeping? No, they aren't. Cut them loose. Your other employees will thank you too. I assure you.

Now, let's move on to the second reason you say you can't let the bad employee go:

2: You have put far too much responsibility on that individual, and as a result... they have you by the throat. You can't run your business without them, and they know it.

Bad move, my friend. In a later chapter, I'll explain how to make sure this never happens again.

Here's an easy fix, if you're managing one of many of your company's business locations (company stores): simply call your district manager, explain the situation, and ask to borrow some help from another store. If you have the opportunity, try to transfer a competent employee into your business, or work to quickly train a replacement. I would also train another person, for good measure, to help ensure you don't put yourself in that position again.

If you're a small business owner, you will have it a little harder, but you need to bite the bullet as well. You'll quickly realize it was the right move, and you may have another employee who will jump at the chance to take the new position.

Remember, leaders take decisive action. Losers delay because they are "afraid of conflict." Suck it up, and just do what needs to be done!

As my late father used to say,

"Leaders don't beat around the bush, son.
They do what needs to be done immediately!"

I also completely agree with the words of that world-renowned philosopher, **Larry the Cable Guy**, when he said, "Git 'er Done!" That's what we're talking about here.

There are far too many fantastic employees looking for a better job today (with you!) for us to tolerate anyone on our team who we know, definitely, should not be there. *Do it now!* Get rid of them.

I'm not saying it won't be difficult. Change is always hard. I like what **Nido Qubein, the President of High Point University in North Carolina** (and another of my many mentors) said about it:

"The only person who likes change is a baby with a dirty diaper!"

Here's my promise to you: you'll thank me later, and you will be kicking yourself for keeping the losers on your team as long as you did. Once you've taken action the first time and replaced your weaker employees, it will be easier going forward. Much easier!

Now, here comes the most frustrating part...

Once you've pruned your weak team members, be prepared for some of your employees to come to you and say something like this:

"We are so happy that you let Bill go. He was a real pain in the butt to work with. Nobody liked him!"

I cannot begin to tell you how many times, over my 35 plus years of management, I've had this happen after I let a troublesome employee go.

In my best Charlie Brown voice, "AAAAAGGGGGHHHHH!!!!"

That drives me crazy! My standard question to my employees is always the same. "Why didn't you say something before now? I'm not a mind reader. If someone is making our other employees' lives miserable, we need to fire them."

To help insure we maintain our strong team, I started a practice many years ago that I have passed on to my managers. Here it is. During the interview process I tell each prospective employee, "I don't care how much money you bring into the company... IF the people you work with come and tell us you're a 'pain in the butt' to work with, you're outta here! Fair enough?"

Of course they always say, "Yes" because they want the job. Go figure!

At this point you may want to ask me, **"So, Dave, just how much of a difference will it REALLY make to my success if I get the wrong people off my bus?"**

There could not be a more apt example of the debilitating effect of having weak, discontented, or subversive people on your team, and the advantages of getting rid of them than the one I heard during my lunch appointment with high school principal Todd Finn and head football coach Kevin Motsinger of New Hanover High School here in Wilmington, NC.

I was so blown away by a story Principal Finn told that I asked him to share it with you. In his own words:

In 2011, I applied, interviewed for, and was hired to become the thirteenth principal at historic New Hanover High School in Wilmington, NC. That is when my life all started to make sense.

That was where the grit of being a homeless teen, the guts of being a combat veteran, the endurance of being a college athlete, the strategic planning of being a college coach, the knowledge of being a classroom teacher, the experience of being an assistant principal in a priority school, and the year of being a high-paced principal at a tiny high school would all come together. God knew that I would need all of those experiences in my toolbox to face what I would go up against at New Hanover.

I knew what I was getting into when I came here. Test scores were down, as well as student enrollments. Crime and violence were up too. The school seemed dirty, to me, during my first tour of the near 100 year old building. But in the eyes of many, to replace the former, life-long principal who had grown up in the area with a transplanted Yankee who had no Wilmington roots and limited experience was a BAD idea.

My reputation for quick turnarounds via hard work and unconventional tactics made those people even more skeptical. I couldn't argue with the notion that for the first time since combat, I was going to be hated and targeted by folks who didn't even know me. The difference is these were not Panamanian Defense Forces, or Republican Guard soldiers. These folks were supposed to be on my team.

From the very first day, teachers who now had to prove themselves to a new principal were folding their arms, standing on the sidelines, and waiting for me to go away so that they could go back to their old ways of doing things: ways that put the school in a bad position. *They snickered during faculty meetings, sabotaged every initiative, and spoke poorly of those who were trying to make our school succeed.*

Meanwhile, other teachers saw me as a breath of fresh air – an opportunity to spread their wings and fly, work hard, and truly make a difference in our kids' lives.

Any success we had didn't matter to the wrong teachers. I must have upset about a dozen of them, because at the end of the year, they organized a secret meeting with board members to have me removed. Sadly, two of my own assistant principals knew about this groundswell of malcontent, and did not warn me until it was too late. I confronted them on this, and was told that they knew about the meetings, but didn't want to upset me. I was puzzled: how did they think I felt knowing that they knew about these meetings all along?

Feeling frustrated and betrayed, I hung in there, and did not leave as they had hoped. Why would I let a bunch of cranky elitists run me off? Panamanian and Iraqi soldiers couldn't do it. God did not bring me this far to allow me to fail at the hands of folks who didn't want to actually work to improve the school. He had bigger plans. Bigger than theirs.

After year one, our results were remarkable. *Fighting had pretty much disappeared, dropping from over three hundred the year before I came to just six last year. Test scores became much more competitive. Dropouts decreased. The graduation rate increased. We won two state championships in basketball and track. Enrollments were rising. Gang activity was disappearing. In fact, the only negative aspect of the school was that fellowship of the miserable teachers, who were quite disappointed to learn that I would return for year two.*

Within the first month of the second year, we were on a roll. Parents were asking for school tours. Open choice students from out of districts were signing up at a record pace. The floors were literally shining, graffiti gone, students were in class, and we were starting to get into a groove.

However, the "Fellowship of the Miserable" struck again.

A petition for my removal circulated amongst the small

group of teachers. *Anonymous letters asking other teachers to join the resistance circulated. Nasty cartoons of my wife and me appeared in teachers' lounges, and unsigned essays were found all over the building calling for a return to the days of yesteryear. Rumors were created.*

My character and faith were constantly attacked. It was mind blowing. People didn't want to be on a winning team if that meant they had to earn their success with me as their principal. They would rather fail. Hatred swelled in their hearts. I turned to God and with my pastors at Life Community Church, asked for His guidance.

My pastors gave me books to read, prayed for us, came to the public school and prayed on the front lawn, brought with them a "Delta Force" of prayer warriors, and never left me feeling alone. Yet, the attacks persisted, as my pastors told me they would. One teacher printed out a litany of emails I sent to the staff—emails that were written out of inspiration from my pastor and his wife as I returned from church each Sunday—and included them in the form of a grievance, claiming that they were painfully long and preachy. That 42-page packet was sent to the school board, as well as the local papers. The board members were great about it. They saw our progress and knew that we were all in for the kids. The newspaper, however, saw an opportunity to pounce.

By the spring of 2013, a young reporter from the local paper caught wind of the "Polarizing Principal" at New Hanover. She began a relentless assault on my leadership style, interviewing teachers anonymously (of course) and running articles based on their side of the situation.

The local news channels quickly took advantage of the opportunity to follow suit. I thought for a moment that I would have to leave New Hanover, and that the "fellowship of the miserable" would win. It was at that time that God made me watch a movie in my mind, of what he put me through to get to this point.

I thought about those couches I slept on as a teen. I thought of the bullets we dodged overseas. I thought about my friends in the Army, who at this point were almost 20 years in, getting ready to retire, having never gone to college. I thought of those long nights in the library. I thought of those games in which I played and coached in college, down by 20 points... only to come back and win.

I thought of the kids I taught, and the 80 or so teachers who did believe in me as their leader. And do you know what? Despite opportunities to start over again elsewhere, I chose to return to Hanover for a third year.

I suppose the pendulum had begun to swing in my favor. Many of the malcontents left by the end of the second year when they knew I was coming back. Some remain, and they continue to sneer and seethe with every moment I remain in office at Hanover. However, their numbers are weakening. In fact, I was able to hire 19 new faces, to include two new assistant principals and 17 other staff members. I had long conversations with each candidate to see where their hearts were before hiring them.

I began to see that God was bringing in folks from my past to battle the resistance to his will at New Hanover, as well as folks from His future plans for our eventual victory for kids. Joining the legion of great educators I already had at NHHS, I believe God brought us all together for a reason."

Update: It breaks my heart to tell you this, but as we go to print... I hear that Principal Finn is leaving our area. Here's his response to my request for additional information on the situation.

"Dave, finding myself incredibly frustrated with a lack of support from above my pay grade, I applied for principalships around the nation. One of the positions I sought was at a brand new high school

in Henry County, Georgia, slated to open in August 2014. I interviewed three times and was unanimously approved by the HC Board of Education in December, 2013.

The decision to move forward in my career was a no-brainer. Although the New Hanover County School Board claimed they wanted change back in 2011, they were unwilling to accept that with change comes dissatisfaction, and that dissatisfaction will result in phone calls from people who reject change. Although the folks who were upset with change remained anonymous, their voices were heard over the needs of the students. I was asked to back down, appease the malcontents, and to "know my place." Simply put, that could not be done. Therefore, I am moving on to a brand new school, to be built from the ground up, and once and for all create the school we have always envisioned.

My next challenge is to create the next generation high school, fill that school with innovative servant leaders, sell this school concept to the community, earn buy-in from all stakeholders, and create a high performing school centered around the individual student. Henry County, GA is on board for innovation and progressive thinking.

I am more motivated than ever to contribute the next chapter to the book of educational leadership. I refuse to lay down my sword in the crusade for excellence in education. While the battle has shifted to a new state with a new set of challenges, I intend to contribute to the comeback of American Education in this ever-changing global marketplace.

Being asked to contribute my story to this book is an honor. But I think my story has a long way to go. The premise, however, is that ferocious persistence in the name of God will pay off. I believe the lives of our kids are worth whatever comes next.

Principal Todd Finn

I'm very sad to learn he's leaving. I greatly admire Todd, and it's simply incredible what he, along with his loyal staff members, were able to accomplish in his first two years here in Wilmington!

Let's examine a few points of importance from Todd's story.

Did you catch the part where his success in turning around the school was so overwhelming that a member of the school board demanded an audit? How about where the local TV station (and newspaper too) wanted to investigate what was going on? Why? Because *radical change is not the norm.* When it happens, it causes people to question HOW it happened. It makes them "uncomfortable."

As you can see, people who only want to maintain the "status quo" will fight you tooth and nail to keep things the way they are. That leads to failure for everyone involved; in this case, the students, and the teachers who truly wanted the kids to learn, are the victims here. This is the end result of having too many of the wrong people on your team.

By systematically replacing the weaker team members who are holding you back, whether intentionally or not, you greatly increase your chances of success.

Here's the good news: the sooner all of your losers are replaced, the faster your personal success will be realized.

Remember, your employees are the foundation of your team, your company. A solid foundation is crucial to your success. Conducting regular recon missions allows you to make sure you have the right people on your team. You won't know who the losers are if you don't, because they tend to fly under the radar until it's too late.

Once you've identified the right people for your team and the ones who aren't fitting, you respond by showing the wrong people the door. Remember, the greatest enemies of your company are not your competitors. They are the apathetic whiners and the inactive malcontents in your ranks.

Recon, Respond, Repeat. Understand?

Let me give you another illustration of the significance of a solid foundation with a story from my own childhood. Growing up as the eldest son of a Baptist preacher, I learned many stories from the Bible.

Hmmm... go figure, right?

Anyway, I remember one particular story about the foolish man who built his house upon the sand. Scripture says "the wind and waves crashed against it... and great was the fall of it." "The wise man," on the other hand, "built his house on the rock, and it withstood the strong winds and waves."

That, my friend, is exactly how you can describe the likelihood of becoming successful as a manager. IF you have a weak "foundation" (composed of the wrong members on your team)... it will constantly undermine your efforts, and you'll have a very slim chance of success. There are no exceptions to this rule. *You, as the manager, are only as good as your people.*

Understand this too: Your people are a direct reflection of you as their manager.

Need yet another reason to listen to what I'm saying here? OK, here's one that impacts your chances for career advancement.

As a manager, you are judged by upper management on the composition of the team YOU have put together. They know that every business rises or falls on leadership. You're the leader, and you control who is on your bus. This foundation determines just how high you will go in your company and industry, more than any other factor. Here's where you might be tempted to say...

"Dave, I didn't build this team! I 'inherited' it!"

Sorry, Sparky! Don't even go there! That's just an excuse!

I think it's safe to say the situation Principal Finn inherited at New Hanover High was something far less than ideal. Yet, look at the results a great leader can achieve in two short years. And that's while fighting against a teacher's union and 50 years of poor management!

People who make excuses and shirk responsibility for where they are in life rarely move from where they are. If that's you, knock it off NOW! You're destroying your chances of having a successful management career and an extraordinary life.

Do you remember what I told you earlier about me wanting to get your attention? Allow me to refresh your memory...

I, figuratively speaking, want to grab you by the lapels, pull you up close to my face, and slap you upside the head while screaming... "Snap out of it!"

Well, this is one of those moments!

Reality Check: If you've been the manager in your current position for one year, or longer, you've had more than enough time to assess, prune, and replace the existing weak members of your team. If you still have the wrong people on your bus, take a look in the mirror... and you'll see the problem.

If this makes you angry... great! There's still hope for you. I didn't write this book to blow smoke up your skirt. Sometimes we need to be irritated significantly enough to force us to take action.

Just like the oyster when it has an "irritant" (piece of sand) enter its shell. It takes action and isolates the foreign material so it doesn't interfere with the health of the oyster. It continuously attacks the piece of sand with layer upon layer of shell material... until it becomes a pearl.

That's my goal for you. I want to irritate you enough to take action on the principles I'm sharing with you in the coming chapters. I want to "polish you up" so I can increase your value to your company!

As I said earlier, "Leaders take action... and Losers don't!"

Here's the good news: YOU get to decide, by your actions, which one you are. Remember... talk is cheap.

There's a quote that I had put on a little sign at the entrance to our offices, so that every employee can see it.

It states...

"I am not paid on my Intentions. I am PAID on my RESULTS."

Results are all that matter.

The late **W. Edward Deming,** known as the "Father of Quality Control," once said, *"85% of your results are determined in the first 15% of any process."*

That could also be said of the top 15% of your employees. You know the ones I'm talking about. They're the employees you don't have to cattle-prod to do their jobs. They're your leaders, your top 15%.

Now here's the bad news...

According to Gallup Consulting's Research,

"47% of your HIGH Performers are looking to leave you right now!"

Did you catch that? I said your **HIGH performers**. Your leaders! Not your pain-in-the-butt losers.

So, why would your best people want to leave you? Because it's been proven, time and time again, successful people will not tolerate working with "lazy, slacker" poor performers. They want out of that situation as soon as possible. They have absolutely no tolerance for people who just want to coast, or just do enough to get by. They want to win!

Here's a perfect example of what I'm talking about.

Take a look at this **12 Elements of Great Managing** list created by **Gallup Research** based on **What Makes Employees Happy at Work**. Please pay particular attention to number 9 on the list. I've highlighted it for you.

The 12 Elements of Great Managing

1) I know what is expected of me at work.
2) I have the materials and equipment I need to do my work right.
3) At work, I have the opportunity to do what I do best every day.
4) In the last seven days, I have received recognition or praise for doing good work.
5) My supervisor, or someone at work, seems to care about me as a person.
6) There is someone at work who encourages my development.

7) At work, my opinions seem to count.
8) The mission or purpose of my organization makes me feel my job is important.
9) **My associates or fellow employees are committed to doing quality work**.
10) I have a best friend at work.
11) In the last six months, someone at work has talked to me about my progress.
12) This last year, I have had opportunities at work to learn and grow.

Once again, **your high performers will not want to work on a continual basis with deadbeats!**

THIS is why it's important to do your recon and respond in kind – not only so you get rid of the losers who aren't doing their jobs, but so you can make sure you keep the winners that ARE.

Let's talk some more about the differences between your best engaged employees, and your worst disengaged employees, and see what the consequences are if you keep your worst employees.

I got this from **Gallup's** website, and it illustrates perfectly the difference:

"The world's top-performing organizations understand that employee engagement is a force that drives business outcomes. Research shows that engaged employees are more productive employees. They are more profitable, more customer-focused, safer, and more likely to withstand temptations to leave the organization.

In the best organizations, employee engagement transcends a human resources initiative – it is the way they do business. Employee engagement is a strategic approach supported by tactics for driving improvement and organizational change. The best performing companies know that developing an employee engagement strategy and linking it to the achievement of corporate goals will help them win in the marketplace.

Gallup's engagement ratio is a macro-level indicator of an organization's health that allows executives to track the proportion of engaged to actively disengaged employees. The average working population ratio of engaged to actively disengaged employees is near 2:1.

Actively disengaged employees erode an organization's bottom line, while breaking the spirits of colleagues in the process. Within the U.S. workforce, Gallup estimates this cost to the bottom line to be more than $300 billion in lost productivity alone.

In stark contrast, world-class organizations that have built a sustainable model have an engagement ratio of more than 9:1 of engaged employees to disengaged employees. As organizations move toward this benchmark, they greatly reduce the negative effect of actively disengaged employees while unleashing the organization's potential for rapid growth."

Did you catch that?

To have a world-class company, you need roughly TEN engaged employees for every deadbeat currently on your payroll.

But, if you're the average US Company, you have approximately TWO engaged employees for every loser on your team. See the problem? That's a huge reason for you to weed-and-replace your current group of slacker "I don't want to be here" employees.

I've had my graphics department create a poster showing the "World Class" and "Average US Company," and the engaged and

71

disengaged employees are depicted as horses and donkeys. It's quite impressive, and we have it hanging in our training room as a reminder for our employees of what we want in our company. You can check that out, and buy one for your company. It's a great way to illustrate the type team you want to build. You can get your own World Class poster at www.Top10Manager.com/Resources.

Oh, and it's not just your employees that you have to pay attention to here. Oh, no! There could very possibly be bad apples on your management team too, statistically speaking.

In a great blog post titled, **"Millions of Bad Managers Are Killing America's Growth,"** **Gallup CEO Jim Clifton**, wrote:

"The problem is, employee engagement in America isn't budging. Of the country's roughly 100 million full-time employees, an alarming 70 million (70%) are either not engaged at work, or are, worse, actively disengaged. That number has remained stagnant since Gallup began tracking the U.S. working population's engagement levels in 2000. Talk about a lost decade.

Why is employee engagement stuck? If you estimate that America has one supervisor or manager for every 10 employees (that gives you 10 million managers) then seven million of those managers are not properly developing, or worse, are outright depressing, 70 million U.S. employees."

Note: I need to meet Jim Clifton one day. I like his style. He tells it like it is!

To sum up, if you want to succeed as a manager, do your recon. Replace weak employees with those who will help make your dream a reality! If they're not FOR you, they're AGAINST you. Period!

Now I've shown you how to fix your team. Later, we will recon your standing as a manager within your district (if you're a company store), or within your industry, if not.

But, for now, let's talk about one proven way we can make sure we have engaged employees. Let's talk about how YOU influence their education.

Let's now move onto the **E** in our

Management R.E.W.A.R.D.S. Principles.

It stands for...

Chapter 4

EDUCATION

Build your people first,
and they'll build your company.

*"You will be the Same Person in Five Years as you are Today...
except for the People you Meet and the Books you Read."*
—Charles "Tremendous" Jones, Motivational Speaker

Over 95% of our nation's managers miss this powerful, career-building principle, causing them to fall far short of the greatness they were meant to achieve:

Educate your employees.

Remember back in Chapter 1 when we said that the NUMBER TWO REASON managers fail is because they don't care enough about their employees?

Educating your employees, or providing opportunities for them to educate themselves, is one of the best ways to communicate the fact that *you care about them*. Think about it. What's the main goal of all parents? To help their kids be the best they can be – to provide for their physical, mental, and spiritual education. It's no different as a manager.

Listen! This is extremely important to your success.

Go back and reread the chart of **12 Elements of Great Managing** (in the last chapter) and you'll find that #6 on the list was: "There is someone at work who encourages my development." That's your job, Sparky!

Need even more proof of the importance of educating your people?

Then check this out: **Jack Welch, the former CEO of GE**, and arguably the most successful CEO in the history of American business, said this recently in an article I read on LinkedIn:

"When you become a leader, success is all about growing others. It's about making the people who work for you smarter, bigger, and bolder. Nothing you do anymore as an individual matters except how you nurture and support your team and help its members increase their self-confidence. Yes, you will get your share of attention from up above – but only inasmuch as your team wins. Put another way: Your success as a leader will come not from what you do but from the reflected glory of your team.

Now, that's a big transition – and no question, it's hard. Being a leader basically requires a whole new mindset. You're no longer constantly thinking, "How can I stand out?" but, "How can I help my people do their jobs better?"

First and foremost, you need to actively mentor your people. Exude positive energy about life and the work that you are doing together, show optimism about the future, and care. Care passionately about each person's progress. Give your people feedback – not just at year-end and mid-year performance reviews but also after meetings, presentations, or visits to clients. Make every significant event a teaching moment. Discuss what you like about what they are doing and ways that they can improve. Your energy will energize those around you.

And there's no need for sugarcoating. Use total candor, which happens, incidentally, to be one of the defining characteristics of effective leaders.

Through it all, never forget – you're a leader now. It's not about you anymore. It's about them."

Jack has the most successful track record, as a CEO and business leader, in American history. I've read every book he's ever written, and he gets it as it relates to management success! And to be successful, you had better get it too!

> *"You don't build a business—You Build Your PEOPLE—*
> *Then Your PEOPLE build the Business."*
> —Zig Ziglar

Remember, your employees must be FIRST!

Then, and only then, will you get what you want.

I do my utmost to live out a "caring about others" philosophy, and I sincerely want you to understand its power, and what it can mean for you. As a result of adopting this belief and mindset many years ago, I am immensely successful. Please don't think I'm bragging when I say that. I just want you to understand what it can mean for your life.

Celebrate learning with your employees. Educate them. Just do it!

It's one of the most underutilized advantages you, as a manager, have at your disposal when building your world-class team. In fact, what I'm going to teach you is rarely ever done within a company's culture.

I have studied this subject for years, and have researched the training programs of many of our nation's greatest companies to verify what I'm sharing with you now. The secret has been around for years, but most managers are too lazy to take action on it.

Here's what one of our nation's founding fathers had to say about the habit of lifelong learning:

"An investment in knowledge pays the best interest."
—Benjamin Franklin

Now, let me clarify something here before we go any further. I'm not talking about your employees knowing and mastering their job responsibilities within your business. Oh, no! Not at all!

What I'm talking about is helping your people take their lives to the next level, which requires some "pruning and watering" on your part as their manager.

No one, and I mean NO ONE, is in a better position to inspire change in an employee's life than their manager, their leader. Typically, the average employee will spend more time with you than with their spouse, family, and friends, so you really see them for who they are.

Why does it matter that YOU take an interest in lives of your team members? Like I said before: *It shows you care.*

"The mass of men lead lives of quiet desperation."
—Henry David Thoreau

That quote describes most people, including your employees, wouldn't you agree? They get up every day, go to work, and as **Michael Gerber** said, they just go about ***"doing it, doing it, doing it... and then they go home each night, and do the same thing tomorrow."*** They get up the next day, and do the same thing, day in and day out.

Yet, they are always longing for something more. They never seem to be inspired to do much of anything, and as a result never become the successful person they were meant to be.

"Some people die at 25... and aren't buried until 75."
—Benjamin Franklin

Does this describe many of your employees? As we learned earlier, **Gallup Research** found, ***"Roughly two-thirds of your employees are 'passively,' or even worse, 'actively disengaged.'"***

In other words, they have absolutely no loyalty to you, or to the company.

You, their manager, have the power and influence (and dare I say the "responsibility" as their leader) to help each of them change their thinking. And I mean ALL of them! **If they go to work for you... go to work on them!** You will never be successful otherwise.

"Leadership and learning are indispensable to each other."
—President John F. Kennedy

This is the point where you have a decision to make. You have the rare chance to be their hero, to cultivate deep loyalty and admiration from ALL of your people, but you have to take action to change the way things have been in your business. Most managers won't, and that's why over 95% of them fail.

So, how do you become the leader you were meant to be? By helping your employees become who they were meant to be; it's as simple as that.

We're talking about getting involved, intimately, in the development of your employees as people (co-workers, spouses, fathers, mothers, friends, etc.). This will greatly improve their success, while also improving and amplifying their contribution to the company's (and your) overall success – a definite win-win for all involved.

I am a student of the game of business, and I am always looking for ways to improve our client's experience with our company, **MyEmployees** (www.MyEmployees.com). That also involves learning what other CEOs in other successful companies are doing.

With that said, our Production Manager, Josh Newkirk, and I recently toured the **Zappos** corporate headquarters in Las Vegas, while attending another trade show. After reading in several business books how great Zappos' working environment was, our mission was to get a better understanding of their corporate culture. If you're not familiar with Zappos, they are the number one online shoe company in the world, and were purchased by Amazon.com for $928 Million.

Though my team and I have been doing what I'm about to teach you for well over eight years, this concept was very recently begun at Zappos the very day we visited. Literally! No joke! Timing really is everything, right? We saw them actually involved in this process, with **Zappos CEO, Tony Hiesh,** sitting at the end of the table (where he should be)... leading the discussion! In fact, if you'd like to see the actual video I took of them together in their conference room while we were on the tour, go to www.Top10Manager.com/ Resources, and you'll find it under "Zappos Company Tour."

Let's continue with HOW this very powerful concept was developed, and then I'll show you how to implement it in your business.

In 1907, **Andrew Carnegie**, arguably the greatest entrepreneur the world has ever known, invited a young newsman, **Napoleon Hill**, to his office one day. He offered him the chance to interview his friends, the top businessmen of their time, so he could find the common success characteristics among these men. Hill was told he would not be paid to complete the work, and would have to pay his own expenses, but he jumped at the chance to sit at the feet of these Giants of Industry.

All told, Hill interviewed 504 people, including Ford, Wrigley, Wanamaker, Eastman, Rockefeller, Edison,

Woolworth, Darrow, Burbank, Morgan, Firestone (and all the great industrialists of the time), as well as three U.S. Presidents.

Carnegie contacted all of his successful friends, and requested they meet individually with Napoleon Hill for a "few hours," but these meetings sometimes turned into days. This entire process, from first meeting with Carnegie when he accepted the challenge to the completion of the book took over 20 years.

The result was Napoleon Hill's 1937 classic, *Think and Grow Rich*, the number one business book of all time, and it is still being read by millions of successful business people today. It has been reprinted countless times over its 85 years in existence, and if you haven't read it, you should get a copy as soon as possible.

It's available on Amazon.com and many other places online.

As you can imagine, during the course of conducting his interviews, Napoleon found many common qualities and success habits exhibited by these leaders of industry.

By his own admission, probably the most important idea Hill learned about when interviewing these Titans of Industry was the concept of the... **Mastermind**.

In essence, a Mastermind is a "brain trust composed of various like-minded individuals who meet for the sole purpose of tackling a pressing problem, or hashing out the merits of an opportunity or idea they are thinking of pursuing." Apparently, Hill found that all the members of this list of famous industrialists were involved, in some way or fashion, in their own Mastermind group, or multiple groups, in some cases.

These Mastermind meetings typically take place once a month, depending on the availability of the individuals

making up the group. However, research has proven that meeting less than once a month diminishes the effectiveness of the process, so it needs to be as often as the members of the group can meet. I've found this to be the case as well in my own groups.

As a successful entrepreneur, or manager, one thing you must constantly be doing is learning new ideas. That's what effective leaders do. Remember, they don't write books about people that stay on the "well-traveled road."

Fact: If you fail to continually learn, you will become "road kill" as new, hungrier, enthusiastic managers come up through the ranks within your company.

Once implemented, this Mastermind concept is definitely something you will be kicking yourself for not getting involved with earlier. Yes, it's that powerful.

I have been, and continue to be, a member of several high-level business Mastermind groups over the years, with membership ranging from $10,000 to $25,000 per year. Like anything else, you get out what you put into these groups. I strongly believe you must always be learning new things to continue to be the best at what you do.

Here's some details about our local Mastermind group I've set up in my hometown of Wilmington, NC. It's composed of five local entrepreneurs, and you have to own a business with revenues of at least $1,000,000 a year to even be considered for the group. We meet once a month.

Since I host the group, I bring my management staff with me. I'm investing the time and money for my best people to be in the room, and that's paid off for me in spades. One of my favorite Bible verses is, "*Iron sharpeneth Iron*." That's what will happen to you and your people, when you have the opportunity to be around other sharp, hungry-to-learn people.

I laugh as I think about it now, because every single member of the group (who I asked to come to their first meeting with us) told me, "Dave, I am a busy guy, and I don't have time to meet with your group!"

Once they starting coming, however, they have never wanted to miss a meeting. That should tell you something of the value these meetings can provide to the group's members and to your career.

Here's one of the guys in our group, **Jon Carne, the Founder and CEO of Port City Apparel** (www.portcityapparel.com), one of the fastest growing "logoed, corporate wearables" suppliers in the country. I'll let Jon tell you himself how our Mastermind meetings have benefited him and his business:

Dear Dave,

I am writing this as I sit at the water's edge in Wrightsville Beach, NC, watching my 14 year old, Jacob, surfing. I mention this because this time of day used to be filled with so many tasks that had to be completed, that I very seldom had the opportunity to spend a weekday morning with my son, my other two boys, and my sweet wife, Michelle. A few short years ago, vacation time, getting away from the office to unwind, and living my life was only a dream, and did not seem possible. Having three distinctly different multi-million dollar enterprises revolving around Apparel supply, manufacturing, and branding, we were staying extremely busy. Too busy in fact. My life was a mess.

Four years ago we were facing some seemingly insurmountable odds with our business, and by extension, it was affecting our family.

What changed the course of my life was God bringing some very wise men into my life, and through their encouragement, correction, and mentorship, I began listening to reason and wisdom.

In January, 2009, Dave Long invited me to his business, MyEmployees, to ask my advice on screen printing some of the metal plates for some of their award plaques. As I was touring their impressive corporate offices with Dave, and his COO, Adam Tartt, my phone was ringing constantly.

Since it seemed we could not carry on a conversation without constant interruption, I could sense Dave was getting a little annoyed with all my phone calls.

I kept telling him, "Sorry, but I have to take this very important call."

After the hour long tour, and our discussion as to the best plan for them, as I was saying "goodbye," Dave gave me an "AHA" moment that really changed my life, and the lives of my family forever. It went something like this:

"Jon, can I give you some advice? You need to get an 'Adam' (his #1, and COO). Adam handles all of my calls that are similar to those you answered today as we were trying to talk. You greatly limit your success and the possibility of ever having a truly enjoyable life if you continue to work like this."

I thanked him for the meeting and his advice, and got into my truck thinking... "Dave does not know how big and important my business is. I HAVE to handle ALL of this MYSELF!"

Then this small voice inside said, "Jon, stop what you are doing, and get a #1 like Dave told you to do."

I called Michelle and said, "I need to get an 'Adam.' I need a #1." OK, honestly, she thought I had finally lost it! She, and others down through the years, had suggested this same thing to me countless times, but I knew best... or so I thought.

That very day we prepared an ad, and two weeks later we had our "Adam" – literally! His name is "Adam," just like Dave said. As you can tell, I follow directions very well. Since that day, we have added several more team members that have helped propel us to new heights we would have only dreamed of before.

So, now that I have given you the backdrop of my meeting with Dave, you will better understand the transformation that we have undergone as a result of our Mastermind meetings. Dave had asked me, several times I might add, to come, and I always blew him off. I did it in a nice way, but I had no plans to go. Seriously, I'm "way too busy to meet with people I don't know, PLUS they don't know anything about my business, and, frankly, it's none of their business what I do in my companies."

But, I finally caved and went. All I can say is, "WOW!"

Honestly, my first few months of our Mastermind were filled with 'resistance and reluctance.' I am not a big change person, so the process of letting folks in to see our weaknesses (and critique our shortcomings) was not something I looked forward to.

I've learned that the single most important decision I can make as the leader of our business is to take action to enrich my 'knowledge base' by systematically setting aside time to read (by myself and as a group), watch videos, and attend our monthly Mastermind Meeting (spending more time with highly successful people). The more time we have spent developing our team, the better our decisions have been, and consequently, our results have started to become predictable.

To sum up what these past three plus years have meant to me, and to my success, is very difficult. Meeting every month with our strong group of entrepreneurs has literally changed my life. These guys understand me, and speak my language.

The opportunity to sit with other multi-million dollar business owners (for four hours monthly) and openly and honestly bring my ideas, problems, fears, and triumphs to the group has changed my thinking forever. We read books and discuss them when we get together. I now have a thirst for knowledge that has set us on a path for massive, continued growth.

Back to the beach...

We just wrapped up a good two-hour surfing session, and now I need to get to my office. You see, I do not want you to get the impression that spending time with my son at the beach was not work related.

As I've learned from Dave, spending this time with Jacob at the beach has cleared my mind, and will propel me into my meetings this afternoon with a true sense of clarity of what is really important for my family and for my businesses.

If you meet Dave you will not forget his energy, sense of humor, and love for the Lord. I hope you take the plunge, follow Dave's advice, and look for strong leaders (and "mentors") to help you on your journey. I did, and that decision (and a lot of hard work implementing what I've learned) has changed our family's path to one of success on so many levels.

Cheers, my friend! I thank God for sending you my way!
Jon

Dave here...

Jon is a great guy, a good friend, and a very successful businessman. Yet, as you read, he was letting himself get distracted from what should have been his main focus with all those "petty detail" calls and emails. His life has definitely changed for the better in the years I've known him, and he's a take action kind of guy who will not stop until he's the best he can be! My kind of guy!

Here's another member, **Robert Rickert, our company's Virtual CFO**, http://rickertcpa.com/, with his thoughts about how he has benefited from being a part of our group:

"I have been attending our local Mastermind with David Long and the other members of our group for the last nine months. In that time, my revenue has increased over 300%. There have been several factors that have led to this increase, but the main factor has been the simple idea of working ON my business as opposed to working IN it. The Mastermind group has been invaluable in helping me accomplish that.*

First, *it provides me a group of experienced business owners and managers to act as a sounding board for my ideas. Their feedback has helped me shape my marketing, staffing, and operating processes.*

Second, *I am able to learn from their successes (and failures), and to take lessons they have learned through experience and apply them to my business.*

Finally, and most importantly, *is the principle that Success breeds Success. Surrounding myself with proven, successful business owners challenges me to rise to their level. I would highly recommend being part of a group like ours to any business owner or manager with aspirations of greater growth and success."*

Thanks, Dave!
Rob Rickert

As you can see from what Jon and Rob shared with us, the Mastermind concept is a very powerful tool when you have a great group of like-minded individuals working toward a common mission. In this case, our mission is to improve our businesses and our lives, but you can have a Mastermind built around any cause, such as building a better community, or participating in raising funds for your favorite charity.

It's that powerful!

You should definitely take it upon yourself (if you really are serious about becoming a Top 10% Manager in your company) to meet at least once a month with other successful managers (whether in your company, or not) and discuss ways, together, that you can create successful, positive changes in your businesses.

So, who do you get to be members of your Mastermind?

Many companies have multiple locations within a 25-mile radius, and those managers are the perfect source to draw upon for your group members. Start there first.

I've provided you the several links below for Creating Your Mastermind reports to help you have a better understanding of how to start your own group, both inside and outside of your business at www.Top10Manager.com/Resources. Scan down the page and you'll see "Setting up Your Mastermind Group". I do not have any kind of relationship with the creators of these reports, but I feel these are some of the better examples I have seen on the internet.

After you've read and listened to these resources, and have a better idea of what needs to be done (such as how to run a meeting), you can then reach out to the others and share your idea of getting together once a month. The reports and the video will teach you what to say. Don't worry about anything. Everything is covered.

Share the video and articles with any prospective members. It will help them understand what you are trying to do, and why they should become a member of your group.

OK, here are some of the ideas you would likely discuss within your monthly Mastermind meetings:

Maybe you're having a problem with a particular employee, and you want to ask the other members of the group how they would handle the situation.

Perhaps you'd ask the group what they would do to fill a vacancy on your management team. You could ask a few of the more experienced members to interview your final few potential candidates, and offer you their thoughts. You never know; maybe one of the group members has someone who they feel is ready for advancement, but they have no opportunities open in their business. You don't know unless you ask.

Having a group of like-minded individuals like this to rely on will potentially save you months of frustration (and untold amounts of wasted money) by promoting the wrong person to your management team.

Here's a little tip for your career advancement: Once your district manager finds out what you're trying to do in setting up your own Mastermind group, you'll be well on your way to being seen as a mover and shaker within your company. Average managers won't take action on following through on successful ideas like this, so it's easy to stand out from the crowd with just a little effort.

Be smart, and don't wait for another manager in your area to read this book first and then call you. If you do that, they will be the one seen as the leader-on-the-move, and not you! You'll have blown the rare opportunity to be seen as an innovative, trend-setting leader in your company. Don't make that mistake. Read the report, watch the video and then pick up the phone, and call the top business leaders in your area, whether they're in your industry, or not. You are going to love this! I'm excited for you to see what I know to be an extremely powerful strategy to propel your career success by leaps and bounds.

By the way, you should definitely be creating a management team Mastermind within your business (and with your top

employees from each department). That's what we do, and it really improves communication between all our departments, and catches most issues before they become problems.

By the way, this does NOT replace your regular managers' meeting. Those are meant to work on what's IN the business. These Mastermind meetings are to discuss ways to work ON the business to improve it. Not to discuss the day-to-day issues. Understand?

If you take the time to implement this Mastermind principle in your business, it will focus the direction of your top employees (and all your employees) into a successful and highly energized team that works together like nothing you've ever experienced before.

Here's a great quote to illustrate the principle of the Mastermind:

> *"Give me six hours to chop down a tree and I will spend the first four sharpening my axe."*
> —Abraham Lincoln

That's exactly what we're doing here. We're working on "sharpening your axe" as it pertains to building your management foundation, and the career foundations of each of your top employees.

Your employees see YOU as the "company" they work for. Research has proven, repeatedly, that an employee's relationship with their manager determines whether or not they are happy on the job.

This bond with your employees, if you trust and implement what I'm sharing with you, is the secret ingredient your career really needs to take off!

You simply must engage and develop the talents of your best employees if you are to become successful yourself.

When an effective employee development/training/ recognition program is adopted and adhered to, religiously, it will be shown to be one of the most impactful strategies you'll ever find in keeping your top people on your team. There's no finer tool to increase your employee engagement as it pertains to getting all your employees on the bus and going the way you want your business and management career to go.

This is not optional if you want to succeed:

"YOU simply must become involved, personally,
in each of your employees' education."

Note: This is not something you can hand off to an Assistant Manager, or delegate to your human resources department. Don't even think about it! They need to see that YOU are concerned for their welfare, and that YOU care enough to become involved and get in the trenches with them. This is huge! Do not miss the significance of this!

PLUS, think about this for a second.

If you are building leaders within your company, as you should be, many of your assistants will be promoted and move on to their own businesses. If they were doing all the training, the employee loyalty that was built with those assistant managers would go with them. Then the employees will still be there with you, and you will basically be starting from scratch in building trust and loyalty.

Don't make that mistake.

For this to have the maximum impact you'll want to experience, you must lead these training meetings yourself.

Remember, leaders lead from the front!

Let me explain why this matters.

Think about your relationship (if you can call it that) with your average employee for a moment. You come into your business, or office, and you probably interact with only a few of your people each day. This can be said about most managers, so I'm not singling you out; I do the same thing many times. It's just the way it is in the average business today.

As you go through your typical business day you focus on the tasks you are required to do, and rely on the other managers and employees to do theirs. Congratulations! You're normal!

But, unlike you (after I teach you these secrets) this is where the other 95% of managers stop. There's so much more to do... IF you truly want to become a Top 10% Manager in your company. You're about to learn how to set yourself apart from the pack!

To do that, you'll simply need to start holding weekly...

Book Club Meetings

"Say what?!! What the heck is a 'Book Club Meeting'?"

Yeah, I thought you might ask that.

We'll get to that in a moment, but first let me explain by telling you how I discovered the power of this principle of "educating my people."

I've always been interested in improving my knowledge and skill set by reading books and attending seminars that I felt would help me become more successful.

It all started when my father, the late Rev. Dr. J.W. Long, Jr., handed me a book by Dale Carnegie, titled *How to Win Friends and Influence People* when I was 14 years of age. He said, "Here, son. This is a great book to help you be more popular at school." Well, who doesn't want that? So I got started on the book right away! Wow!

Excuse me, I meant to say "WOW!!!" because it was that powerful! The lights really came on for me.

I distinctly remember how reading that book helped open my eyes to certain principles of dealing with other people, and how I could improve my relationships with practically anyone.

When I finished it, I immediately reread the highlighted portions I had just marked so I would not forget anything. It was awesome! If you've never read the book, please put it on your list immediately. It's a classic, for sure. It will amaze you as you study and truly learn how people think.

Dale Carnegie's book was the first of many hundreds (if not thousands) of books I have read, and I continue to read several books every week. Having started on the quest to never stop learning, I find myself feeling rather unfulfilled each day if I don't read for several hours. I literally have "reading withdrawals." I can't possibly tell you who the latest Hollywood sensation is, but I can doggone, for sure help you build your business, and increase your chances of success!

All right, let's continue with my story...

Approximately ten years ago, I read a book by my friend, Dr. Tony Zeiss, titled *The 12 Essential Rules for Becoming Indispensable.* (Dr. Zeiss is the long-time, highly successful President of Central Piedmont Community College in Charlotte, NC, the largest community college network in the country, and I am indeed fortunate to call him my personal friend and mentor.)

After reading and highlighting his wonderful book, I knew I had to share what I had learned with my own employees, so I ordered them each a copy.

And that, my friend, is how our Book Club meetings began!

I called a brief meeting with all employees, handed out the books, notebooks, and a highlighter to each of them and said,"I want you to each read chapter one of this book by next Wednesday at 11:30. As you read it, please write your thoughts down in the notebook I gave you, and come prepared to talk about what you, personally, got from this chapter. I will have pizza delivered so we can enjoy lunch together as we share what we learned with each other."

Crickets...

Dead silence...

Nothing but blank stares coming my way...

Get the picture?

OK, so not everyone was jumping up and down with joy and loudly cheering, "Dave, that's an awesome idea!" when I told them what we would be doing.

Nope!

In fact, several of them were rumored to be rounding up the villagers, with torches and pitchforks in hand, searching for the evil monster who came up with the idea!

Oh, believe it or not, it gets worse...

About ten minutes after our meeting had adjourned, two of my rather introverted employees privately came into my office together, and told me they were "uncomfortable talking like that in front of others." I listened, thanked them, and replied, "I appreciate the fact that it makes you uncomfortable, but you're among friends here, and we all be will sharing, so relax and enjoy our time together as we eat lunch and learn as a team." They reluctantly said they would try, and promptly left the office.

I'm definitely not going to sit here and tell you my Book Club idea was accepted with open arms. **It wasn't**. By the way, rarely if ever, are things that make you successful easy to do, or implement.

Then the day finally arrived for our first meeting...

OK, I'll admit it! During our first Book Club meeting, people didn't know what to expect. They'd never done anything like this before with any of their former employers, and the last time they were in a reading group was the fifth grade, and let's just say they did not remember it fondly! They definitely had reservations as to exactly just how much they felt they could share, but, as we ate our pizza, I set the example for our group by sharing stories from my own past to help reduce their anxiety.

That first chapter of Tony's book happened to be on *Attitude*, so I shared a story of how having a negative attitude had affected my life for a few years after losing a job. I wanted them to see I have been-there-done-that too. I showed them I was human, and I had made many mistakes along the way.

Sometimes I shared things my siblings and I had experienced growing up as preacher's kids. After hearing my stories, it seemed there was always someone ready to share their story.

Then, it happened...

One by one, each member of the group felt compelled to speak up, and began to open up about themselves and their experiences in life. It was fascinating to see how it just started to flow out of them. We laughed, and sometimes even shed tears together, as each chapter reminded us of stories from our own lives.

By the fourth week or so, every employee's reservations to share had all but completely evaporated.

What we found was we were coming together as a team. People, who had historically ignored employees from other departments, soon established new friendships. Some even started doing things together away from the office, such as going to the gym together.

During our Book Club meetings people shared their humorous (and sometimes not so humorous) stories from their childhood, and how it related to the chapter we had read that week.

Many times we recounted how something we had perceived as a disaster in our lives turned out to be a wonderful blessing. Some team members had been kicked out of their homes, or left because of an alcoholic, abusive father or mother only to tell us how that experience had forced them to grow up.

Occasionally, you could glance around and see others begin to get a little misty-eyed as someone recounted their personal struggles in life. OK, I'll admit it. I did myself a few times too. Hey, I'm human!

As an example of our sharing our stories with each other, I explained how we would not have been sitting there eating lunch in our break room that day, if I had not been fired many years earlier.

I shared how I went through seven jobs in three and a half years, lost everything and then, at the age of 31, had to pack up my wife and three children and move back in with my parents. I asked them, "How many of you have had to admit defeat, and move back in with your parents with your spouse and children in tow?"

Not one single hand went up.

They started to say things like, "Wow, Dave, I had no idea

you went through all that!" They had a newfound respect, and empathy, for me as their leader. I was sharing my heart, and I was forming a deep bond with my people. In essence, we were becoming "one"!

Oh, yeah! I almost forgot to tell you this. Remember those two employees that came into my office and said they were uncomfortable sharing and speaking in front of the other employees? Well, after only a few weeks, one of them came and said, "Thank you for making us participate, Dave. I would have hated to miss these meetings, and if you would have made it optional, I would not have come."

Remember this:

"A great leader will take you places...
you would never have gone on your own!"

You are taking your people, sometimes kicking and screaming, to places they never would go in their lives, and they will remember you forever for it. Let me show you some proof of that... talk about perfect timing!

Here's a very touching comment I received from one of my former employees (from many years ago) named Drew Crosby. I noticed on LinkedIn that he had taken a job as ski instructor and golf pro at Crested Butte Mountain Resort in Crested Butte, Colorado, so I sent this short note of Congratulations to him.

Living your dreams, son! I'm very proud of you, Drew!

Dave Long

And here was his very kind reply to me:

Thanks, Dave!

I couldn't have done it without you. I constantly talk about your open, honest, efficient, but simple approach to business. You made me interested in what goes on behind the scenes, and because of the books you had us read, I have made myself indispensable. Not many ski instructors around here have real estate investments, retirement planning knowledge and half a year's salary in savings.

So, thanks for your mentoring. It did not fall on deaf ears!

Drew Crosby

I'm sure you know that Drew's comment meant a great deal to me. I printed his message, and added it to my personal "treasure chest" of heart-felt notes I've been collecting for years. In fact, my employees gave me the chest, a few years ago, for Christmas. In it they each placed a heart-felt message telling me what I have meant to their lives. Let me just say this. If there was a fire in my house I would grab the family pictures, and then I would grab my "treasure chest." That's how much the cards and letters of my employees, family and friends mean to me. I'd probably grab my wife in there somewhere too! Ha!

Think about this: I've read that Mel Gibson has won 29 motion-picture-related awards. You probably think I'm crazy, but I wouldn't trade Drew's or any of my employees' personal messages for all of Mel's awards!

I have hundreds of comments from employees, former employees, friends, and family telling me how the time we've spent in our Book Club meetings, or the advice I've given them, has changed their lives. Man, that's inspiring to me!

Yes, these Book Club meetings are powerful, but ONLY if you make them happen with YOUR team.

Here's a little more of what you can expect when you open up with your team:

When you share, they share.

As soon as you dismantle, brick by brick, that false wall of separation (between yourself and your employees) and allow your employees to get to know the real you, that's when the magic happens. The changes are subtle, at first, but you'll see the welcomed progression as time passes, and as you share more about yourself and your mistakes (and the lessons learned) in life.

If you recall, I mentioned earlier that I ordered pizza (or sub sandwiches) when we began the Book Club meetings. It's a very small outlay of cash, but it gives a huge return on investment. Knowing that, you may be confused by what I'm about to tell you.

I no longer buy lunch for the employees when we hold our Book Club meetings.

About now, you're thinking...

"What? You cheapskate! Why would you stop buying the pizza?"
We stopped because, as we grew together as a team, our company began to grow at an even faster pace (adding more and more employees), and we could no longer hear each employee's thoughts on a particular chapter each week. There simply was not enough time.

Also, sometimes employees' personal lives (such as doctor appointments) caused them to miss the lunchtime meetings. Something had to change. The whole purpose of WHY we were holding the meetings was to bond together as a team and hear each other's input. Anything that prevented that from happening was unacceptable.

Now, if you think buying the pizza was more than you wanted to spend on my idea, and you've already decided you weren't going to do it anyway...

Listen Up, Sparky, and get prepared for a HUGE Shock! Though I stopped paying for lunch...

I started PAYING every employee to be in the Book Club meetings for an hour EACH WEEK!!!

Yep, I paid them all, while still on the clock, to sit in a room with me for a whole hour every week!

"Oh, Dave, you've lost your ever-lovin' mind, son! There's no stinkin' way I am going to PAY my people to sit in a room for an hour a week instead of doing the work they're getting paid to do! Not a chance!"

Remember the Abraham Lincoln quote I shared earlier? Here it is again...

"Give me six hours to chop down a tree
and I will spend the first four sharpening my axe."
—Abraham Lincoln

To maximize your career potential, it's imperative that you spend sufficient time sharpening your biggest, most efficient, and impactful "axe" (your employees) FIRST... before anything else is done. If you fail to do that sufficiently, you'll never reach your full potential as a successful leader.

However, if you invest the time needed to help develop their skills—and show them they matter to you enough to spend quality time to help them become successful in their careers—there's no limit to how high your career will soar! The beautiful thing is, you'll do it together, working alongside each other as you work to improve your lives and incomes. This one hour spent together each week amplifies the work accomplished in the other 39 (if they're full-time employees). Quit thinking "short-term," and start thinking of the long-term benefits you'll get by implementing my Book Club Meetings in your business.

Please, I beg you, do not allow the small investment of time and money to dissuade you from doing this. That would be a huge mistake, and these Book Club meetings will pay for themselves many, many times over in the coming years of your management career. I assure you!

Remember this, because it is a Universal (and Biblical) Law:

"You Reap what you Sow"

What we're doing with our Book Club meetings is planting seeds of greatness in your people, and ultimately in you. If no seeds are planted by you, then you should expect no harvest! Stop thinking as if today is the only day that matters. It's not. This is a long-term strategy for success. Seeds take time to grow, and that's what we're going to do together as we grow your team.

Note about paying for the books: Since most companies have "employee training" factored into their budgets, you should talk to upper management, tell them what you are doing, and ask them if the company can pay for the books for employees (roughly $10 per employee, every two and a half months – if the book has ten chapters).

Think about this for one moment! As expensive as it is to replace just ONE of your top employees, explain to your DM why they should fund this endeavor. Everyone, and I mean "everyone" benefits from these Book Club meetings, so it's worth asking them to help you with the expense.

"But, Dave, what if upper management balks and says they won't pay for the books needed?"

That's easy to fix! Buy them yourself and tell the employees that you are "paying for the books because you want to help them in their lives, and in their careers." This is huge! They will TRULY believe that you care if they know YOU paid for these books.

I can hear it now, *"Dave, I have 100 employees, and these books cost around $10 each! That's $1,000!!! No way am I spending that!"*

Yes, it is about $1,000, but let's think about this for a second. There are book "alternatives" today that were unavailable to us ten years ago. Have you heard of Amazon's "Kindle" books? If your employees have their own computer, the Kindle download is free. They just have to pay for the books they download.

OK, before you completely pass out from the lack of blood to your brain or have a panic attack after reading the $1,000 price tag, let's take a moment to look at the reality of what you'd actually be investing as a manager.

One great source for books (I purchase thousands of my books from them every year) is **Tremendous Life Books** (www.tremendouslifebooks.org).

They have an "On Sale" page where you can buy many book titles for $3.00, or less, per book. This is an excellent (and very inexpensive) way for you to start your own Book Club meetings. **I highly recommend Tracey Jones and her fine team. I have used them for years**. Talk to them; tell them how many books you'll need for your business, and they'll work with you to fit your budget and recommend some great books for your team. I assure you, they will take extremely good care of you.

A great book they have (as of this printing), and a book that will positively impact the lives of your people, is Jim Rohn's, *The Seasons of Life*. My employees really seemed to like that book too. Last time I looked, Jim's book sold for $3.00. See, I've already got you down to $300!

Try to plan to spend some time on their website, and look at all the options you have for books to read together. You'll be glad you did.

Being a small business owner, I started out exactly as I am telling you to do. I only had about twelve employees at the time, so I ordered a copy of Dr. Zeiss' book, *The 12 Essential Rules of Becoming Indispensable*, for each of them.

This is an excellent book to start your Book Club meetings with, and you can order as many copies as you need for $12 each (including S&H) from: charlottetownepr@bellsouth.net. Note: If you order the books in quantity, you'll get a much better price per book than $12 each when you order. Just tell them how many you need for your team.

Here's another great option: I just checked on Amazon.com and **Dale Carnegie's classic, *How to Win Friends and Influence***

People, is only $8.40 for paperback, and $7.98 for the Kindle version, if your employees have a computer, iPad, or Kindle Reader. See, your options are unlimited!

Book Club Schedule

OK, let's examine how you go about setting up a schedule for your employee Book Clubs.

Let's say you have 100 employees in your department, or business. Obviously, like my business today (at MyEmployees, with over $8 million in annual sales, and over forty employees on staff), you'll need to divide up your team to effectively get to know each team member personally.

We currently divide our company up into two groups (with about 21 members per group) with one half of the employees coming Wednesday morning at 10:00 am, and the other half the same time the next day.

Now, if you have a larger amount of employees, splitting your company into two groups is probably not a good option. If that's the case, split your team into three, four, or even five Book Club meetings a week. But, please remember the whole point of these meetings is to "build the team as a whole," and help them bond with you, their manager, and with their fellow employees.

Oh, I can hear you now! *"Dave, I don't want to spend four to five hours a week in Book Club Meetings! I have a business to run!"*

Fair enough, but may I remind you that your number one responsibility as a manager is to increase the sales and profits of the business you manage. When you're successful in building a stronger, more bonded team, you're pretty much guaranteed more sales, personal income, and more promotions! Your goals can ONLY be accomplished by motivating your employees to do their best.

Remember, you can move a giant object quite easily when using "leverage." That's what we're doing here by motivating, engaging, recognizing and rewarding our team members.

Earlier, I shared with you Jon Carne's experience with our Mastermind Group. Well, after learning of our company Book Club meetings, he (eventually) listened, and started holding his own with his team.

Here are his comments about the experience:

"Dave Long suggested doing a Book Club for our office for months, so I finally relented in 2012, and said I would. We chose a book recommended by Dave's Sales Manager, Melanie, called **The Ultimate Sales Machine** *by Chet Holmes.*

Honestly, I think everyone in my office was waiting to see if this was for real, or a "flavor of the month" reaction to the daily grind we were going through. Each week I asked for a chapter to be read, and then we would take two hours every Thursday to discuss what we read. It was great to see the very in-depth conversations, and "give and take" among the entire staff. I saw attitudes change as we learned things about ourselves (and each other) that really shed light on what we brought to work every day how they either positively, or negatively, impacted our work and results in life.

Over the past year we have completed another three books on Leadership, personal development, learning processes for success, and dealing with change. I cannot believe the change in the attitudes of my team and, most importantly, the accountability we all have for making sure we are communicating effectively, and doing the best job possible for our clients."

OK, did you catch the last part of what Jon said? He mentioned "doing the best job possible for our clients." Pay careful attention to that, because that is what gets us the success we want.

Fact: The more you do to improve the skills and attitudes of your people, the better they will take care of your clients and customers. Higher sales and profits will take care of themselves when that's accomplished. Seriously! Wake up, and as I said, *"Quit thinking short-term."* Remember, we're planting seeds, and they take time to grow into an abundant harvest of superstar employees.

Can you imagine how much easier your life will be when you have a team working like that for you?

Think AUTO-PILOT!

Another key point to remember is to mix/change up your Book Club group members every few months. This allows the groups to get fresh new ideas from other team members they have not been able to share with for a while. It also helps make sure every employee gets to know the other employees beyond just the first name they see on their name badge.

Also, make sure a variety of employees from each department are grouped together. This will greatly improve the camaraderie between departments, like nothing else you've ever seen.

With this strategy of smaller, more interactive groups, you'll be fulfilling the responsibilities of taking excellent care of your clients and customers, and at the same time, employees from each department will always be available to help your clients or customers. After all, that's why you're there.

By the way, your Book Club meetings will greatly enhance your employee engagement and customer service scores too! I've seen it happen time and time again. I remember one **Best Buy** client manager telling us his *Employee Engagement scores went from #22 in his district to #7 after only a few months of using our company's engagement and recognition plaque*

program.

That's music to my ears!
Speaking of Employee Engagement, you may want to ask...

> *"Why does it matter whether, or not,*
> *my employees get to know each other?"*

Because it's been proven, over and over again, "If you have several good friends (or even one) at work, you're less likely to leave that job for another one."

Let's do what we can to help build loyalty between our employees, to ourselves as managers, and ultimately to the companies we each work for.

I can't wait to hear what happens when you begin educating your employees by holding your Book Club meetings. Expect to see leaders emerge in each group, and prepare to see, first hand, how some of your more quiet employees (and even some new hires) will handle their time in the limelight.

It's genuinely empowering to see them growing right before your eyes. Please send me a note and let me hear the feedback you get, and how you're helping people change their lives! It will make my day, I assure you!

Now let's move onto our next chapter where it really gets exciting! You'll begin to see your Winners Emerge. You'll really see how your newly implemented Book Club strategy will be a huge contributing factor in developing your future business (and company) leaders.

So, let's get started!

And now, let's move on to the **W** in my

Management R.E.W.A.R.D.S. Principles.

Our W stands for...

Chapter 5

WINNERS EMERGE

"Regard your soldiers as your children, and they will follow you into the deepest valleys; look on them as your own beloved sons, and they will stand by you even unto death."
—Sun Tzu, *The Art of War*

To me, one of the greatest by-products of the deepening relationships you'll foster with your employees in these Book Club meetings is the incredible growth you see in their lives. The closest thing I can compare it to is watching flowers bloom. It's extremely gratifying as a leader to see your people begin to grow and change their lives right before your eyes.

Speaking of "eyes," please don't roll yours, and laugh that statement off as hype. It's not!

In fact, I'd like to invite you to come experience our Book Club meetings, first hand, if/when you're in our area. We'd really love to have you come participate in one of our discussions. We just had Bill Willetts, the Regional Sales Manager for *Snap-on Tools*, attend the other day.

The book topics change all the time, so there's no telling what topic we'll be discussing on any given day. I'm a stickler for having "well-rounded" employees, and you only get that by learning about all aspects of their lives.

Our weekly discussion may be on personal finances after we watch a DVD of Dave Ramsey's *Financial Peace University*. Or, maybe we will talk about having a better relationship with our spouses as we read the Carnegie classic I mentioned earlier, *How to Win Friends and Influence People*. You never know with us. That's also part of the excitement! Keeping it fresh is very important.

If you'd like to come, please contact my office, and we'll set that up for you. As I said earlier, "I'm here to help you become a Top 10% manager in your company." I'm completely committed to your success. You've invested in my book, and you deserve no less from me.

OK, let's continue with the changes I've seen in the lives of my employees.

Through the years, I've seen many employees show immediate change, while others, being suspicious at first, took longer to grasp what was happening to them. Regardless, the suspicions melt away after a new employee has been exposed to our culture for a short while.

Your best people (your winners) will love these Book Club meetings because they'll have an opportunity to "shine." People will respect them. Many of them have never experienced that unique feeling before, so they'll appreciate you for making that happen for them. Opportunities will arise through promotions, and these people will be ready for their chance! You made that happen, and they will always remember that.

Now I want to tell you a little about **Adam Tartt**, our COO (Corporate Operations Officer), who is arguably the finest, most loyal employee I've had since I started the company 25 years ago. In order to show you what Adam means to me, I need to take you back to the Civil War era again.

Let me set the scene for you...

The Battle of Chancellorsville was probably Lee's and Jackson's finest victory of the war. Despite facing an army twice their size, Lee strategically split his forces, and sent Jackson around the Union flank. This was a surprising move that the Union Army of the Potomac was certainly not expecting. The result was the most stunning defeat of the war for the Union Army.

When nightfall stalled the attack, Jackson and a few of his aides rode forward to survey the area for another possible assault. But, as they rode back to their own lines, a group of rebel soldiers from North Carolina opened fire. As I said, it was dark, so these soldiers assumed they were Union soldiers since they were approaching their lines from the front.

During the volley of "friendly fire," General Jackson was shot three times with .57 caliber bullets. One of the Southern bullets shattered his left arm, which ultimately had to be amputated the next day. He also cracked several ribs when his aides dropped him while attempting to carry him to safety. As he lay in bed recovering from his amputation, pneumonia set in.

Jackson quickly began to fade.

Being a devout Christian, he died (as he had wished) on the Sabbath, May 10, 1863. *"Let us cross over the river and rest under the shade of the trees."* Those were his last words.

I tell you this touching story to share the finest compliment Lee ever bestowed upon his favorite, and most effective military officer, General Thomas "Stonewall" Jackson.

Upon hearing Jackson had lost his left arm via amputation, Lee tearfully said, ***"Thomas has lost his left arm... and I have lost my right."*** In my opinion, there is no higher, more sincere compliment one man can bestow upon another human being than this.

And with this story still fresh in your mind, I want to say that Adam Tartt is my "right arm," and I love him as a son. Being far more than an employee to me, he is my most trusted confidant, and I always know he will look after our employees and our clients almost as well as I do.

As my number one team member, I've asked Adam to take a few moments and share his story with us, so you can get an idea of the type of employee you want on your team.

Adam, his sweet wife, Bekah, and their girls.

Here's Adam's story in his own words...

When Dave asked me to tell my story, I've got to be honest, I was a little overwhelmed. I mean, I have been with this company for a long time, so where do I start?

*After I had a chance to reflect on my past successes and failures, I realized that it wasn't all that complicated. It was not my intelligence, my stunning good looks, or electrifying personality. No, what I wholeheartedly believe was and is the "key" to my success here and anywhere else, is one word: "**ATTITUDE**."*

Now that you know the key to success in everything in life, resist the temptation to stop here and close the book because you have it all figured out. Humor me with enough time to prove it.

I was raised to value hard work. My father is one of the hardest working people I know, and that is something that has stuck with me my entire life. My grandfather (now in his eighties) still gets out every day, climbing ladders, crawling under houses, and fixing toilets.

I took my first job when I was 14, which was a catering gig that involved 12–14 hour days on some weekends. There was a time in high school when I was actually working three different jobs while going to school five days a week. So, it is safe to say that I had the right attitude about hard work instilled in me from an early age.

However, the attitude of working hard isn't everything. It isn't even the most important thing. I began to develop the attitude of wanting more – no, wanting to BE more.

Also, what I would eventually learn from Dave is: If I wanted to "EARN more... I had to BECOME more." I had to want to be better tomorrow than I am today.

I started working for Dave in November of 1997, during what I thought was a seasonal help situation. When Dave asked me to join his team, I thought it was your typical trophy shop, and he just needed some help to get through the holidays.

I was wrong.

What I found was a small company that thought BIG. The reason this was so revolutionary to me, was that I was used to working for a big company that thought very SMALL.

At the time I came to work for Dave, I was working for a national grocery chain, a local gym, and teaching martial arts at an after school program in town. I knew coming to work for MyEmployees would mean I would have to cut at least one of these other jobs loose.

It was an easy choice.

You see, everyone talks about how teachers, police officers, and firemen are the faceless heroes, the behind-the-scenes professionals that are egregiously underpaid but even more pitifully under-appreciated. While I certainly tip my hat to those noble professions, I take exception to the above referenced platitude. To those that would make such a statement, I would simply ask, "Have you ever worked in a grocery store?"

Okay, so in an effort to restore any shred of credibility I have left after making a statement like that, let me explain. Working in a grocery store, or in any type of retail environment, is extremely unrewarding work – for those who work hard.

I remember an event from my first week on the job, as if it were yesterday. I was a bagger for a local grocery chain, and one evening we were particularly slow. I was moving from register to register, cleaning the belts, loading plastic bags on the stands, emptying trash, etc. My thought was, "I am on the clock – I can't just stand here and do nothing." However, to my surprise, nothing was exactly what my front-end supervisor wanted me to do. I remember my manager, Jeff, saying, "Adam, slow down. Just hang out up here and talk with the rest of us."

I was surrounded by status-quo employees, wanting nothing more than status-quo results in life. I wanted more than that. When I started as a bagger, I wanted to learn to be a cashier. When I was a cashier, I wanted to learn how to run the dairy department, then the receiving department, and so on.

I had a hard time working for a company that did not notice or recognize that "fire" in me.

To make matters worse, the pay was embarrassing, and you can forget about getting a raise simply because you worked harder and had better results than anyone else. No, this was a company, like many others, where its employees were simply cogs in a wheel, gradually spinning around and around until the next "annual review" came around. If you were "lucky," you would get a whole 20 cents raise for your blood, sweat, and tears for the previous year.

Don't get me wrong, I was thankful for my meager, or should I say, VERY meager raise. It was just frustrating that it was the same raise that was given to the guy who used to sleep in the dairy cooler for half his shift, and never smelled quite right.

Believe it or not, that wasn't the worst part. The fact that they never said thank you hurt much more than not being paid what I felt I was worth. When companies operate that way, they are missing the boat entirely.

As you can imagine, it was easy for me to leave that company when another opportunity came around. They had no problem giving me more responsibility because they knew I would treat it like my own. However, they had a HUGE problem in showing me appreciation. I was never recognized, systematically or spontaneously; never told I was appreciated, either formally or informally.

Working for Dave has been an entirely different experience! Our company has room to improve just as any other does, but I know that we recognize and appreciate our employees more than any other company I have ever worked for.

I know what you are thinking "Of course you guys recognize your employees! You sell Employee Engagement and Recognition Programs!" I guess you could say, we practice what we preach. And that is what motivates me. I get to see the faces of the folks that are recognized, and know what it means to them. (If you go to www.MyEmployees.com/stories, you'll see what I mean.)

Here's something that I find very interesting: The very team members that manufacture the Employee of the Month plaques for our clients, bubble over with pride when we bring them in front of the rest of the company to say how much we appreciate them going above and beyond, and explain why THEY earned Employee of the Month. If there was any group of employees who you think would not be excited about receiving their plaques, it would be them. But, they are just as excited as anyone else.

Being recognized for your achievement and hard work never gets old, even for an "old-timer" like me that has worked in this industry for over 15 years.

Dave doesn't stop at recognition. He has done more to develop me, educate me, train me, and mentor me than you can imagine. After having graduated from a great business school, I can honestly say that I have learned more about business and life from my time working with Dave, than I could have ever learned in college. I will never be the same, and for that, I am eternally grateful.
Thank you, Dave.
Adam Tartt
Chief Operations Officer
MyEmployees.com

I swear – every time I read that my eyes well up with tears. As I've touched Adam's life... he's touched mine. As you can probably tell, Adam spoke from the heart, and I know he means what he said. That's the thing about working and growing with people every day, they get to know the real you, warts and all.

Don't miss what he shared with us.

There were three distinct and very powerful "Management Lessons" in Adam's story.

They are:

    1. **Recognize excellence in your people, or they'll leave you for someone who will**, like Adam did.

    2. **He hated working with "status quo" employees.** (AKA: Losers) Note: Remember Gallup's research, where they found "47% of your BEST employees are looking to leave you right now!" Just like Adam, they can't stand to work with incompetence, and will not tolerate it for very long.

    3. **Adam wanted MORE... and he wanted to BECOME more**. He had ambition, and wanted to excel at what he did, and wanted to become a leader.

Adam found what he was searching for in all THREE of these critical factors when he came to our company. That's why he's still here after 15 years.

So, what did you learn from Adam's story? Hopefully, you will see why you want to find (and foster the growth of) this type of employee.

Employees like Adam are the key to your success. Without developing your own Adams, your foundation will never be strong enough to support your life's ambitions, dreams, and goals.

If you recall, this chapter is titled, Winners Emerge. Now, let me tell you about how Adam stepped up (AKA: emerged), showing me I had a winner (and definitely a Keeper) on my team.

Some things I noticed early on about Adam: He was always on time. Not only that, but if we got busy, he would stay late to help get the job done without being asked! Thankfully, we rarely need to ask people to do that, but he had the attitude: If I'm needed, I'm there! He also exhibited character, and he was respectful to me and all the employees, regardless of their age, job title, or their time with the company.

Let me inject a very powerful management lesson for us here.

During our weekly Book Club meetings, I have a few sayings I like to remind everyone of (my employees sometimes call them... **Dave-isms**).

Here's one of my more legendary ones...

"Would you say to the fireplace, 'Give me heat, and then I'll give you some wood?' Of course not!

"Would you say to the field, 'Give me crops, and then I'll give you some seeds?' No way!

Then why would you say to your employer, 'Give me more money, and then I'll work harder for you?'"

Sorry, it doesn't work that way.

Adam planted the seeds and put the wood in the fireplace FIRST to earn the opportunities that would come his way later.

Little did I know his opportunity would come sooner than he (or I) ever thought it would.

Here's what happened...

I had a young man who was our production manager at the time. I won't mention his name, as I would not want to embarrass him. So, let's just call him "Bill."

Bill was really a great employee... until he got married. He and his wife were amateur collectors. Barbie dolls for her, and sports memorabilia for him.

Though I paid him very well, Bill and his wife managed to get into $40,000 worth of debt in a very short time, mostly credit card bills. I didn't know there was a problem until he came into my office and said, "They are coming to pick up my truck!" I said, "What?!! I pay you very well, son. What the heck are you doing with the money?"

Bill went on to tell me about their expensive hobbies, and how much trouble they were really in. (Several truck payments, and several credit card bills, to name just a few.) Against my better judgment, I offered to loan him $1,800 to catch up his past due bills (with no interest for six months), and told him to get his act together. As you can probably guess, he took the money. What a shock, right?

Well, as you can probably imagine... nine months went by, and not one, single, solitary word about my money.

Oh, it gets worse...

It just so happened, at about this same time, I had to go to the doctor (where his wife was employed as a receptionist), for a routine physical. As I was being checked in (by his wife, no less), I noticed one of our company's custom-designed walnut desk plates on her desk. These were designed specifically for our company, and are not available anywhere else.

I thought to myself, "Funny, I don't recall Bill (her husband) buying one of those from me."

Hmmm... interesting.

When I returned to my office the next day, I called this employee (our production manager) into my office for a little... pow-wow (as my father used to call these type meetings).

I asked him about the money he owed me, and reminded him that I didn't charge him any interest as a way to help him. He immediately went on the defensive, and started to defend his lack of responsibility in paying me back.

Let's just say, he had a *tone* that was unappealing.

Then, after he had basically blamed me for his lack of character, I brought up the "desk plate situation." I said, "Bill, I was at the doctor yesterday where your wife works, and I couldn't help but notice that she had one of our custom-designed desk plates on her desk. Correct me if I'm wrong, son, but I don't remember ever selling you one of those. That means you took it without my permission."

Oh, and as they say, "It was ON like Donkey Kong," baby, after that revelation!

Bill screamed at me, "So, I guess I'm a thief now, is that right?!!" I simply said, "If it walks like a duck, and talks like a duck, son, it's probably a duck!" He immediately stormed out of my office, and disappeared into the back of the building (into our production department).

The next thing I know, he's darting past my door, personal things in

hand, on his way out the front of our building, all without saying a word! I got up from my desk, and immediately went to see if he had said anything when he was in the back. All he told them was, "I quit," with no explanation, and simply left.

In his defense, Bill came back in a few hours later that day, and presented me with a check from his mother for my $1,800 loan plus a "little extra" for the deskplate. There was never any admission of guilt, as you might have imagined, but there was no need. The additional funds told me what I wanted to know.

Pretty soon, after Bill stormed out, the reality of my situation started to settle in, and I realized, "I just lost my production manager. Bill was one of the most vital employees in my company. What do I do now?"

Like any business owner worth his salt, I sat down and quickly analyzed the predicament I found myself in. Like you, if you've ever been in the same situation, I started to assess the capabilities of my existing employees. It didn't take me long (with only six or seven employees at the time) to realize that my options were limited, to say the least.

In this case, as I will show you, that was a good thing. Because, if I would have had other more logical choices, I would not have made the decision I did. Thank God for that!

Do you recall what I shared with you a few pages ago: "Would you say to the fireplace, 'Give me heat, and then I'll give you some wood'?" I was referring to our employees delivering the goods before expecting more money (a raise) from me. Remember that?

Well, that is how I came to make the decision of WHO I would talk to first.

With my "firewood before expecting heat" scenario firmly

in my mind, I went straight to Adam, and asked him to come into my office.

Let me give you a little background here before we go any further, so you fully understand the complexity of the situation I had before me. Adam was a 19 year old sophomore in college, a full-time student. Because of school, he was only working about 20 hours a week with me during this time.

Despite this, I had really been impressed by the fact that he seemed to work all the time, just like I did when I was in high school. Few people his age would be working even one job, much less three. I saw a lot of myself in him, and I wanted to encourage his ambition and desire for growth.

When he started working for me, he was planning to get a business degree with an emphasis in finance. He would ask me questions about sales, leadership, and management. Our conversations would turn to different books I had found beneficial, and I gave him full access to my personal library of hundreds (now thousands) of books.

I also saw Adam take my advice when he asked for it. On one occasion, as he and I were riding in his truck to pick up a piece of furniture I had purchased, we got into a discussion about his proposed housing plans for college. He mentioned that he and his friends were going to get an apartment together near the school. Being a successful real estate investor, I immediately said, "Why would you want to get an apartment, Adam, when you can get your own house?"

To say that Adam was giving me the deer-in-the-headlights look is a slight understatement. But, as he listened, I could tell he was intrigued by the idea.

With this visibly perplexed look on his face, I went on to explain the

tax benefits of owning his own house, and how the other two young men could help pay his mortgage. I showed him how, with the tax savings, he could, in essence, live rent-free. Plus, when the time came to get married, he could simply kick the two guys out, which is exactly what he ultimately did.

Let me interject a little snag that came up with my buy-your-own-house suggestion for Adam. Did I mention that he was only 18 at the time and just starting college? Yes, I believe I did! His parents, being hardworking, protective, wonderful parents, were not too thrilled that ol' Dave had suggested this to him. They tried to talk him out of it, and if I recall correctly, his dad even called me with his questions and concerns. But, with some solid numbers I gave him to show them, and their knowledge of the fact that he was a sharp, reliable young man, they relented, and helped Adam buy his first home.

So... Adam bought a house at 18 years of age! How many of you reading this right now can say that? I know I can't.

The boy actually listened to me! Imagine that, a teenager actually listening! WOW! OK, I'll settle down now, and get back to the story.

Wait! Did I mention that he actually listened to me?!! That's wild! OK, "Down, Psycho Dave, down! You have a story to finish!"

Here's the key ingredient to Adam's success. Over the two years that he had been with my company, Adam had proven himself to be (though a very young one) a man of responsibility, character, and integrity. Three critical qualities needed in all your leaders.

I knew what kind of man Adam was. And that is the main reason why we were talking that day.

I shared my dilemma, and I said to him, "Adam, I would not even be talking to you right now except for two things: you have been an extremely reliable employee since you've been with us, and you've always listened to what I have told you."

I went on, "Son, you know Bill has quit unexpectedly, and that leaves us without a production manager. We have to have one, and I want your opinion on something. Here's the deal. You are the most dependable employee we have in your department. Because you are the best of the group, I want to offer you the chance to choose from the two options I'm about to give you.

"The first choice is this: you can become our new production manager. I think you would do well at the position, and I know I can trust you to get the job done. I realize you've still got a few years left in college, so this will not be easy. But, if you can promise me that you will work no less than 30 hours per week, the job is yours.

"The second choice is this: I will hire Bill's replacement, you will teach him or her how to do everything, and then he or she will become your boss! Which one do you choose?"

I'm sure you'll agree this is a lot to put on a young college kid but, as I said, Adam was no ordinary, "let's see what I can get out of doing" college student. Not by a long shot!

Upon hearing my options, Adam immediately said, "I want the job!" Now, that's the kind of quick decision a leader would make, and it showed me I was making the right choice. None of that "I need to think about it" drivel.

That's the kind of employee you can build a solid career foundation upon as you help your people build theirs. As I've said, "Adam is my right arm."

Think about your existing team. Do you have your own "Adam" on your team? If you're blessed, maybe you have several, like I do.

124

Here's another story about one of my winners emerging. It further illustrates what you should look for in your people.

Yuichi Murakami is our IT/Web Director, and he's been with us for approximately seven years. (His name is pronounced "U-E-CHE.")

As you can probably tell from his name, Yuichi is of Japanese descent. The Japanese are a very reserved people, and when I asked Yuichi to submit his story for my book, well... I could tell he was not too thrilled about the idea. But, after I told him I wanted to celebrate him and the job he does for us, he reluctantly agreed.

Here's Yuichi's picture. He's an avid kite surfer, and this is a cover photo from a local magazine. He's pretty proud of that, as he should be!

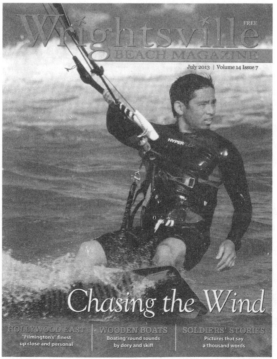

Here's Yuichi's story in his own words:

Born in Japan and raised in Brazil, I would say I've grown up with very unique (weird?) experience. Even though I was born in Japan, our family moved to Brazil when I was a very young child, so growing up, I actually felt as though I was more Brazilian than Japanese at times. Maybe that's why I am a very confused individual! Just kidding.

I was raised in a traditional Japanese household, and respect was something I was taught as a very young child. Also, being involved in martial arts at a young age has taught me to respect others, especially elders, and to be humble. However, even though my parents and many of my life experiences have taught me core values about the significance of hard work, I would say the true lesson, or "eye opening," came later on in my life, in my twenties.

Before joining MyEmployees, I have to say I was in a very interesting place in my life. I had moved to the United States at age 18 on my own, without any of my family. Luckily, the school I attended in Brazil taught me English as a third language. While living in Rhode Island, over the next several years, I pursued music, which was my dream. Just about every evening I would work as a music producer until midnight, and sometimes until 3:00 am.

To make enough money to pay the bills, I also had a job working as a customer service agent at a local car rental agency. My work days started at 8:00 am, and typically ended around 6:30 pm, Monday through Saturday.

I was also the car washer on the coldest winter days, many times when it was 20 degrees outside. In addition to that, I was also a part-time mechanic. Changing tires, oil, and fixing various car maintenance issues on the cars was also my responsibility. During inclement weather and snow storms, I also made myself available to shovel the rental cars out from under several feet of snow (by 2:00 am), so that the vehicles would be ready for business after the storm.

Looking back, one thing I can say is that even though it was not pleasant work, I did it. I just knew that I had to do it, so I did. I don't want to say I am a hard worker because I really didn't think it was hard work at the time. It was just unpleasant.

My father has always taught me that to be a leader, you must first know how to be at the bottom. So, subliminally, I think I was living the "bottom" my father talked about. I am sure my father never wanted me to live the life I've lived, or experienced, but I would say that this time was very important and gave me some of the best life lessons I've experienced/been taught in my life.

Without it, I would have never ended up in North Carolina and met David Long and our MyEmployees crew.

Dave always tells us, "You have to be ready and prepared for the opportunities that come your way." That definitely has come true in my life! Even while working long hours at the rental car agency I continued studying web design, and worked on many other projects that I hoped would move me closer to my dreams. This extra studying is what ultimately provided the skills for the position I now have.

The story of how I came to NC is rather interesting. I had met Josh, David's son, when he was in New York trying to break into the music business. We became friends, and he introduced me to his father when he visited our area. The rest, as they say, is history.

Since I have been working at MyEmployees, my life has completely changed for the better. I have learned to really pay attention to details, and I always try to contribute more than is expected. It has paid off for me. Coming from nothing, to being *able to own my own house, is just unbelievable to think of when I consider where I was before coming to MyEmployees.*

It may sound corny, but I'm living my American Dream. Not only do I now own a house, but I also recently became an American citizen!

As I mentioned before, being born in Japan and growing up in Brazil, I never knew where my home was, but I did find it finally. My home is here, in the United States, in Wilmington NC. and with MyEmployees.

Thank you very much, Dave, for all the lessons you and the company teach, and all the recognition you give us.

Yuichi Murakami
IT/Web Director
MyEmployees.com

As I said earlier, the Japanese are a very reserved people, so please allow me to share the important details Yuichi, being the humble guy he is, left out.

As he said, I met Yuichi through my son, Josh. As a father, we always try to support our children in their dreams, and my son's dream (at the time, and much like Yuichi's) was to be involved in the music business.

Josh and Yuichi had become good friends, and when we decided we would expand our business onto the web, Josh (who had since moved back to NC) started telling me about this friend he'd met in New Jersey. He told me how Yuichi was "self-taught," and that he had created some great websites.

As it so happened, Josh and I went back up to New Jersey for a real estate meeting, and Josh asked Yuichi to go to dinner with us.

During that meeting, I was very impressed with Yuichi, and asked him to join our team. I agreed to pay him more than he was making, with the understanding I would increase his salary when I started to make money from the web traffic sales he would generate. I spent over $120,000 that first year to send Yuichi (and Adam) to various training seminars, and to pay for the hardware, computers, etc., that we needed.

Discovering that the people searching for employee engagement and recognition online is rather small, we realized it would be many years before we recouped the investment in Yuichi, the needed equipment, and the website expansion.

Now, here's where Yuichi began to shine as he took a perceived negative, and turned it to his advantage.

Having seen that it would take years to pay for himself through online internet sales, Yuichi took it upon himself to learn the technical maintenance on our new, recently purchased, $100,000 Cisco Phone System. There were two huge manuals, and Yuichi took them home and read them. Personally, I would have slit my wrists during chapter one! Talk about boring reading! In the end, Yuichi became the go-to-guy expert on our phone system.

Oh, but wait! There's more.

That was not all he did!

Yuichi also took it upon himself to be able to update, backup, and expand our proprietary client database. Before he mastered database updates and maintenance, we had to pay someone $125 an hour, so Yuichi found yet another way to save the company money.

If Yuichi were an average employee, he would have found "busy work" to do until we fired him for not delivering on

what he was hired to do. But he's anything but average. He's the type of "dig in and get it done" employee managers need on their team to be successful today.

Though it was not his fault, because he did everything we asked him to do, the internet sales did not materialize as we'd hoped. That did not stop Yuichi from delivering far more value than I had asked of him in the beginning. As a result, Yuichi makes nearly three times his starting salary today, and is one of our best, most dependable team members.

Though my son, Josh, may feel that his venture into the music business did not work out, from that experience I gained Yuichi, one of my finest employees. It has definitely been a win for me, and I believe (based on his own story) for Yuichi as well. We are indeed fortunate to have him with us.

As I did after hearing Adam, I want to point out... **Three Principles from Yuichi's story**:

1) **He was working on his dream (music and web design) WHILE employed in a job he did not like.**

2) **He was spending time teaching himself how to create websites on HIS time.**

3) **He made himself invaluable to us by learning about our phone system and database maintenance without anyone pushing him (or paying him) to do so. Again, on his own time.**

That is what separates the winners from the whiners. Can you begin to see how having team members like Adam and Yuichi will make your job so much easier, and dramatically affect your success as a manager? Yes, I believe you can.

When you find these diamond in the rough employees, begin the polishing process, and you'll simply be amazed at the priceless gems you'll find just waiting for their chance to shine.

A final note about polishing your diamond employees: When you find and begin to develop these diamonds, it automatically adds immense value to the other diamonds on your team as well. Remember what I shared with you earlier from the Bible: "Iron sharpens iron." This definitely applies to having superstars on your team.

Example: In the case of hiring Yuichi, he made Adam's life "sooooo much easier" (Adam's description) shortly after bringing him on board.

Before Yuichi joined our team, Adam was our in-house IT tech/mechanic/phone/database/Jack-of-all-trades guy.

Those were not his strengths, and certainly not the best use of his time. But, Adam was the most tech-savvy member of our team at that time, and we had no choice but to involve him in whatever needed attention. Yuichi, loving "all things geek," freed Adam up to do other things that added far more value to the company. Net result: A definite win for everyone!

That's the beautiful thing about hiring a whole team of superstars. They all work in harmony to make each other better at their jobs. The collaboration between them when discussing a problem, or an opportunity we're thinking of pursuing, is a beautiful thing to see. Make sure you remember this as you build your own team.

Never, ever settle for mediocrity from yourself, or from your people. Don't stop grooming your best employees, and replacing your weak team members, until you get an entire team of winners!

Trust me! When you get a team of superstars, your district manager (and possibly corporate officers even higher) will take notice! They'll know you are a leader with the right stuff.

Now let's move on and examine the one characteristic found in ALL superstar employees, and I believe this is the most important piece of elemental DNA that you need to search for in your people (current and future). If you don't get this right, your efforts to be successful will suffer.

That brings us to the **A** in our

Management R.E.W.A.R.D.S. Principles.

Chapter 6

ATTITUDE

*"NOTHING can stop the man with the right mental attitude
from achieving his goal; NOTHING on earth can help the
man with the wrong mental attitude."*
—Thomas Jefferson

My dearly departed father (whom I loved and miss so much) used to use this illustration in one of his sermons.

Here's how it goes...

The old town drunk was asleep on a park bench in the town square. Two mischievous teenage boys, with nothing better to do (go figure), decided they'd have a little fun with him, and waited for the old drunk to fall asleep.

As he slept, they stealthily crept up to him, and one of the boys gently kneaded a clump of Limburger cheese into the underside hairs of his scraggly, matted, unkempt beard.

(Note: If you've never smelled Limburger cheese... well, it flat out stinks, kiddies! I mean, it's the kind of stink that makes you throw up a little in the back of your throat!)

After a while, the old drunk woke up, looked a little perplexed, and crinkled his nose a few times as he sniffed the air. "Whew-ee, it stinks here!" he said as he stumbled to his feet to search for another, more pleasant place to sleep.

He quickly sighted another bench nearby, hobbled over to it, sat down, and took a big whiff of the air around him. "Man, it stinks here too!" he exclaimed. He wondered aloud to himself, "Hmmm.... maybe it's the city?"

Deciding he needed to get some fresh air, he gradually worked his way out into the countryside. But, because he was unknowingly carrying the nasty smell with him... he found no relief from the dreaded stench.

Eventually, the old drunk climbed to the top of the nearby mountain, reared back, took the deepest breath his old lungs would allow... then gagged, and nearly threw up! He screamed in an angry tone, "Man, the whole world stinks!"

I love that story because it is a perfect illustration of what having a sorry, good-for-nothing, rotten, the-world-has-done-me-wrong attitude will do to your life. It doesn't matter where you go, what job you have, or what relationship you're in. If your attitude stinks, the "whole world stinks" to you!

Here's a great illustration of someone who suffers from this Attitude Affliction:

There's a friend of mine who, God knows, I love dearly, but he blames the world, continually, for where he is in life today. You probably know someone like him yourself. He used to be flying high (by the world's standards) but made a series of ill-advised, devastating mistakes that cost him his career and his former, much more comfortable lifestyle. Everything he does, or becomes involved in today, eventually seems to turn into a crap sandwich.

As I have seen him interview for, get, and then lose various jobs, one thing is always consistent: his sorry I-know-better-than-these-idiots attitude follows him everywhere he goes. There's no escaping it. He has, in essence, some of the "Limburger Cheese stank" on him, and he apparently loves the smell, because he doesn't seem to put much effort in washing it off. Note: Yes, I meant to spell it "stank" because the word "stink" doesn't accurately convey just how devastating having a bad attitude really is to your success.

Regardless of where he goes… my friend takes his "stank" attitude with him!

For some strange reason, the movie *Caddyshack* (with Rodney Dangerfield) just popped into my mind as I sit here writing this, so I guess I'm going to chase a rabbit here. Or should I say… gopher?

"AHEM." Sorry, I couldn't resist. If you saw the movie, you just had a little laugh with me there. Admit it!

Do you remember the scene when Ted Knight's character, the snobbish, nose-in-the-air judge, was getting ready to putt (for a lot of dough, I might add) in the competition he was having with Rodney Dangerfield's character? Anyway, the putt he was about to make was for $40,000! Right before he was to putt, he requested that his grandson, Spalding (who was acting as his caddy) hand him his prized putter, "Billy Baroo."

Ted carefully takes the protective sock-type sleeve off his beloved putter, snuggles Billy Baroo up close, kisses it, and then whispers, "Oh, Billy, Billy, Billy."

The scene is on our resources page if you can't remember it:
www.Top10Manager.com/Resources

In my mind, that's how my friend coddles his misery and the stink that goes with it. Just as Ted lovingly held that putter up to his lips, my friend also gingerly nuzzles his old, trusted friend (his bad attitude) every day. Because he's had an intimate love affair with it during the last few years, it's now become a part of his DNA, if you will. Something drastic will have to happen for him to wake up from his self-induced, miserable, self-pity fest!

That starts with his decision (that's all it is) to change his… ATTITUDE!

All he (and maybe someone you know) has to do is decide to take a bath and "get the stank off of them." The number one thing he should do is accept responsibility for where he is today, and take positive steps to escape the pit he has kept himself in for several years.

He's not alone in his thinking, by the way. I was there myself 27 years ago. I had to force myself to change my attitude.

Notice I didn't say it was easy. Change, my friend, rarely is.

It's time for him to quit whining, and start winning again! He's been a solid performer in the past, but he's simply lost his way. I'd continually tried to help him, but in the end, it was up to him to change his attitude.

A word of caution: if you know someone like this, be careful. Do what you can to help them stay positive, but beware. As they say, "Misery loves company," and such a friend will turn you into a complainer too, if you stay around them too long. Guard your attitude for what it is... the foundation upon which your success will be built.

Geoffrey Chaucer, known as the father of English literature, was quoted as saying that the *rotten apple ruins its neighbors*. Get the idea? You need to be alert, so you will notice if your friends help reinforce your positive attitude or try their best to destroy it.

Whether you're a rich man, a pauper, a success, or a failure, there is one thing you have complete control over... and that's your Attitude.

Everything you think about, and everything that happens to you during the day, goes through your personal Prismatic Attitude Filter.

You know the one I'm talking about. You use it every day.

Maybe a disgruntled customer chewed you out for messing up their order, or perhaps you were blessed when your district manager listed three pages of things in your business you need to correct when he made his unscheduled visit today. Oh, and he wants them all fixed by next Tuesday! Been there, done that one, too.

I think you'll agree that your prism through which you look at the rest of the world is slightly darkened after such a day.

And then, on your drive home it gets even darker. You start asking yourself, "Why is every moron in the city driving ten miles below the speed limit in the LEFT lane?

AAARRRGGGHHH!

Why are these people even allowed to breed?"

And then, with your anger (AKA: "sweet spirit") swelling within you, you hit the door of your house and begin to share your newly acquired good nature with your spouse, who merely grunted as he or she realized you were home.

And then it happens...

You go to sit down, and you realize your dog has upchucked on the carpet right in front of your easy chair!

AAAARRRGGGGHHHH!

Oh, and then, "It's ON, baby!"

"Katy, bar the door!"

You start finding fault with, "What's for dinner?" and "Why are there millions of pieces of Lego toys" your three-year-old son has scattered across the room and, of course, the old family favorite, "Where the heck is my TV remote?" (OK, sorry. That one hits a little too close to home for me, and my wife might see this, so mum's the word on that one, OK? Pinky swear? Great! I owe you one.)

OK, I've forced "Psycho Dave" back in his cage for now, so we're good.

Bottom line: EVERYTHING about your life stinks IF your attitude does.

If you have some of that "Stanky Limburger Cheese in your beard, or in your hair" you're the only one that can get it out.

Now, before you totally tune me out, and say to yourself, "Dave, I've heard this, 'you've got to have a positive mental attitude' bunk a million times, and I'm not interested in this 'rah-rah' junk! I'm going to skip ahead to the next chapter."... DON'T!

Pay attention here, Sparky! This is another one of those "grab you by the lapels and smack you upside the head" moments, so listen up!

American Philosopher, William James, speaking on the subject of our Attitude, once wrote,

"The greatest discovery of my generation is that a human being can alter his life by altering his ATTITUDES."

Did you catch that? He said the **GREATEST discovery** of his generation. Could that be right? Absolutely, it could!

President John F. Kennedy had a very positive, "We can do this!" attitude when he declared, in the early 1960s, *"America will put a man on the moon by the end of this decade!"* Though he didn't live to see it personally, his dream (and dare I say, "goal") was realized.

Let me ask you, What did President Kennedy know about aerospace engineering? Not a cock-eyed thing! He, along with all the world's population, saw the Russians put the first rocket into space, and he took immediate action to propel our space program past the Russians by the end of that decade. He led the charge in making the goal of putting a man—an American man—on the moon a reality.

That's what having a positive "we can do this" attitude will do for your career. That's the attitude of a true leader, and if you (and your management team) fail to have the right attitude, how can you expect your people to?

This is one of those foundational principles I mentioned earlier that you must grasp if you're to become a successful, Top 10 Manager in your company.

I believe this quote sums it up better than any other; I tell my team this one all the time:

"A truly great leader... will take their people places they would NEVER have gone on their own!"

Isn't that what Kennedy did? Yes, it is. His dream required focusing the efforts of our space program's scientists into one, specific goal: A man on the moon by the end of 1969.

Would our NASA scientists have said we would put a man on the moon by the end of the decade? No, they wouldn't and they didn't. In fact, when Kennedy made the statement, these scientists cringed, because they didn't believe it could be done.

Here's another great quote, this time from **the Bible** (Proverbs 29:18):

"Where there is no vision the people perish."

Where there is no leadership in YOUR business, every- thing and everyone will perish. Write it down! It's up to you to lead. It's your responsibility to set the vision for your business. That responsibility cannot, and should not, fall to anyone else. Accept the responsibility, and deal with it.

William James also wrote this...

"It is our attitude at the beginning of a difficult task which, more than anything else, will affect its successful outcome."

That's where you are now, at the beginning of a difficult task. You're going to shake up your business and team, and solidify your "launch pad of success," so your career will take off to new heights!

James also said this...

"The greatest weapon against stress

is our ability to choose one thought over another."

You will have moments when you're frustrated, but you must persevere. Your income and potential career accomplishments depend on it.

What should be the most well-known quote related to our attitude (and how it affects our future results) is:

> *"Your Attitude, NOT your Aptitude,*
> *will determine your Altitude."*
> —Zig Ziglar, Motivational Speaker

Have you ever wondered why they write books about the heroes and not the vanquished? I remember learning the answer to this question many years ago, when someone bluntly pointed out to me, *"Dave, the victors write the history books."*

Hmmm... good point!

So, remember, it definitely helps your chances if you're a winner. When you're leading your team, you had better have the proper winning mental attitude found in all great leaders. Otherwise, you are destined to fail.

> *"Whether you think you can, or you think you can't,*
> *you're right."*
> —Henry Ford

Call me crazy, but I seem to remember the children's book being titled *The Little Engine that Could*, instead of the "Little Engine that got frustrated, gave up, and went home!" It takes both confidence and persistence to be successful, and sometimes it seems like both tanks are pretty close to empty.

I've been there myself, where I've thought about quitting a few times in my life. I remember one such occasion back in 1990 (a mere 24 years ago), a little more than six months after I started my company. It literally seems like it was yesterday!

Here's that story:

I was traveling the Southeastern United States at the time, and happened to be in the beautiful city of Orlando, Florida. I had been showing my employee recognition awards programs to retail store managers, real estate brokers, restaurant managers, car dealership managers, and others all over the city for three and a half days, from 9:00 am to roughly 8:00 pm every day, and had sold nothing. Not one single, solitary thing!

This had never happened to me before, and it was the longest dry spell I had ever experienced (before or after). *It was seriously wearing me (and my increasingly fragile confidence) down in a hurry.*

Side Note: Now, for you young whipper-snappers who can't go through ten minutes without checking your phone or texting your BFF, this was back in the Stone Age before cell phones were very popular (or affordable) and when long distance calls at a payphone cost 25 cents a minute. Sorry, but unlike E.T., I wasn't able to just "phone home" and talk to my wife for very long for my much needed moral support. I simply couldn't afford it.

Oh, did you catch the part about where I was making NO SALES? *Zippo! Nada! Goose Egg!*

No money was coming in, but it was rapidly disappearing from my wallet! I was spending money every day for a hotel room (let's just say Motel 6 was really "living large" for me), three meals a day in restaurants (mostly fast food), and gas to get down there, driving around the towns where I was working, and getting back home again. Unlike our free-spending government which miraculously prints all the funny money they need, my funds were limited and dwindling fast. Very fast!

Yep, I felt like I was on my own against the whole, "No, we don't want any of what you're selling" world. After three and a half days of nothing but "No! No! No!" I was starting to lose my confidence, and was saying, "Lord, did you really want me to do this? Maybe YOU made a mistake." I'm embarrassed to admit it, but these actual words came out of my mouth.

Well, you didn't think it was MY fault, did you? Seriously! The gall of you people! Ha!

It was just me out there... alone. I seriously thought about quitting, but I didn't. *I fought back the negative, defeatist thoughts, and continued with my mission. Oh, and I prayed really, really, REALLY hard.*

It just so happened, I was at a Sam's Club on Orange Blossom Trail at about 11:00 that Thursday morning (see, I told you I remembered everything!), and I was showing my award plaques to the manager of the store. He and several of his management team were loving what they were seeing, and I started to get excited! My pulse quickened; I started to soar into the clouds, and then I had one of those "Hold on there, Mr. Enthusiasm! Let's get back to reality!" moments when the manager said, "I love your plaques... BUT I can't make that decision."

Blam! Blam! Blam! "Mayday! Mayday! I've been hit, I'm all shot up, both engines are on fire, and I'm going down fast!"

Yea, that's about what it felt like. Depression. Totally! I had one of those "I want to slit my wrists, and I really want to make it hurt so I'm using a butter knife!" moments.

And then I heard these blessed, angelic words come out of the manager's mouth a few seconds later: "The district manager's office is upstairs. Will you come up with me to show these to him?"

"Well, of course I will!" I said.

Jubilation! Suddenly the clouds parted slightly, and the angels were humming quietly. Not singing, mind you, but they sure sounded like they might be warming up for it.

The store manager and I, who was clearly excited enough to do the talking, ran up the stairs like two giddy school girls to meet with the district manager. Fortunately, we all had a great conversation together, and the DM was very excited by what he saw. My little plane was keeping its nose up, the flames were going out, and I had begun to turn toward the heavens again.

After showing him the program and explaining to him how the store manager could use the program to increase his sales and profits, he turned to me and said, "I'd like this program for all TEN of my stores!"

"Wait! That's a $3,250 order!" I thought. "Is that angels I hear singing? By George, it is! And it's the Hallelujah Chorus no less!

"Hallelujah! Hallelujah! Hallelujah!"

Let's just say at that particular moment in time, I know I had a terrible "poker face." I was very excited, but tried my best to keep my composure. I failed miserably. I would have been wearing Depends that day if I knew he was going to say, "Yes, I want your programs for TEN stores!" I did not see that coming.

And then it happened! A sickening feeling swept over me when I realized that this was a really large order for my very young company. I realized I would have to buy hundreds of plaques up front and then wait for a few months to be paid. I couldn't do that. I knew it. As I said earlier, this was a $3,250 order, and I couldn't possibly pay anywhere near a third of it up front just for the plaque boards themselves, much less pay my one employee (besides my wife and me) to help us make them and ship them.

A little history here. My sweet wife, Janet, and I had lost everything a few years earlier after I lost my job, and we had totally destroyed our credit. *A series of failed jobs had left us with next to nothing. In a little over a year, we had wiped out all of our savings. Several yard sales did little to help the situation.*

In hindsight, I should have taken unemployment, considering we had three children in grade school at the time. But, being the eternal optimist, I didn't. I knew I would get a great job soon.

Bad move. It didn't happen.

We sold our house two weeks before it was scheduled to go into foreclosure, and ultimately had to move back home to Carolina Beach, NC, into my parent's 1,340 sq. ft. home. That's where I started our now $8,000,000 employee engagement and recognition business, in a 5'x5' space in my parent's non-air conditioned garage.

Back to our story...

As I said, I had no money to fund the purchase of the plaques and brass for ten stores, and no line of credit. My parents had no money to loan me either. I told you my dad was a pastor, so you know he didn't have any money. I had already pawned my watch and ring a few times to pay for a C.O.D. (cash on demand) plaque shipment to fulfill several orders, and to pay my one employee during those early months. You can assume I know what it means to barely get by financially.

With all of this going through my mind, I stood in front of the district manager and the store manager. I said, "Guys, this is a larger order than I normally make at one time. I will need to buy hundreds of plaques upfront, wait for them to come in, engrave them, ship them to each of your ten stores, pay my labor costs, and then I'll have to wait 30 days, or more, to be paid. I will have a hard time doing that right now. Is there any way I could get some money up front to help me cover the initial expenses? Please feel free to call any of my existing clients (as I laid down my binder exposing all my clients' business cards inside for him to see), and they'll vouch for me delivering on my promises."

Then I waited for the bad news... but, thankfully, it didn't come.

The angels started "singing" quite loudly when I heard the district manager say, "That's not necessary, David. Would you like half of the money up front?"

"Yes, that would be very helpful and appreciated!" I said. And with that, I packed up my plaques, and we all walked downstairs to the manager's office. Once there, the district manager and I continued *our conversation as we waited for the manager to return with half the money for me. When he returned, he counted out sixteen, $100 bills and some smaller bills, too!*

Cue the Angels again, Baby! Sing it with us...

"Hallelujah! Hallelujah! Hallelujah!"

If you would have put me in a ring with Rocky Balboa at that moment, I would have kicked his steroid-enhanced butt! OK, sorry, Stallone! I may have been a little overzealous with that comment, but hey, I was pumped! "Dun, Da, Da, Dun, Da, Da, Dun, Dun, Dun!" Sorry, that was the Rocky Theme playing in my head! I'm telling you, it really felt great to have a huge weight lifted off my depressed spirits and my beaten-down, drooping shoulders.

I forgot to tell you something. When I first said I was starting my company, my Dad had said, "Do your awards business on the side, son, and get a real job." I can't tell you how good it felt to know I would NOT have to face him (while nursing a bruised ego, and with my tail between my legs) when I got home. I never wanted what he called a real job again, and I never had another did-I-make-a-mistake-starting-this-business? moment again.

As I walked out of the Sam's Club, with my sixteen $100 bills in hand, I said what I always said after making a sale.

Thank you, God, and what a country!

Oh, and right after that, I headed over to Daytona Beach (about 40 minutes away), drove my old Honda Accord out onto the sand right next to the water (it's what they do there), parked my car, looked around to make sure nobody could see me, put on my shorts in the back seat, and then ran into the ocean screaming "Work day's over, baby!"

What? Not what you were expecting?

Are you thinking I should have kept my nose to the grindstone and made more sales calls that day? No way, Sparky! Not that day. I needed a mental break after my nearly four-day sales drought was over. I'm only human, so cut me some slack! I'm not Superman; though I do have a pair of Superman boxers! Hey, don't judge me! My wife bought them for me. You're just jealous! Deal with it.

OK, enough about my Superman skivvies. Let's get back to business.

I'm sure, as you look back over your own career as a manager, you've had days similar to mine where you were on the edge of quitting, but you didn't. You persisted.

Why?

Because when you were just an employee you obviously did much, much more than the average person was willing to do, and that made you stand out to your manager. That's how you were first noticed. You excelled at a much higher level than the others around you (some who had been with the company much longer than you had), and you were rewarded for that.

Why?

Because your manager saw something special in you. That's why. They recognized your positive "I'll do what it takes to get it done" attitude.

Here's one thing I have noticed down through the 35+ years I have managed people. That type of attitude is not the norm today. Indeed, it's very rare in this "I'm entitled, and you owe me" environment we find ourselves in today.

Think about the people you know who've been promoted in your company. Ask yourself, "What kind of attitude did they have about themselves AND about the company?" I assure you, they believed in themselves and in the company they work for. I'm willing to bet that describes you too.

If you really have the desire to become a truly successful Top 10 Manager, you have to lead by example. Double-check your attitude every day! Make sure yours is worthy of emulation.

And now, for the second **R** in our...

Management R.E.W.A.R.D.S. Principles.

Chapter 7

RECOGNITION

*"The Deepest Principle of Human Nature
is the Craving to be Appreciated."*
—William James

Note to ALL Managers who fail to properly recognize excellence in their top employees:

If you don't believe, as a business manager, that employee recognition matters to your employees because it's no big deal to you personally, then please allow me to say...

"Thank you! Thank You! THANK YOU!

A million times over I say, **"THANK YOU!"**

If you would have shown each of your employees—someone like David Strange, our Top Salesperson, over all, for the last four years (and someone I'll introduce you to in a second)—the proper recognition he SHOULD have received, he, and many others like him, would probably still be working for you.

You're not alone. We've all lost some great employees because of some bone-head mistakes we've made as managers. Myself included.

Listen up, because here's the real world situation we find ourselves in as managers today:

Every employee you have is either a Patriot or a Mercenary.

I forget where I read that, but let's look at the characteristics of both:

Your Patriot Employees:

- Are loyal to you and to the company.
- Know you genuinely care about them, and they appreciate you in return.
- Are shown appreciation when they do a good job, and are rewarded for it.
- Bond with other employees in the company, and have many friends there.
- Believe, and support, what you're trying to do as a manager.

(These employees drank the Kool-Aid. As someone once said, "They will follow you as you charge into hell with a water pistol!" OK, that might be a bit over the top, but you get the idea.)

Your Mercenary Employees:

- Are there for themselves entirely, so there's no loyalty to you, or to the company.
- Don't care about you, and they don't believe you care about them either. Hence, no loyalty.
- Receive no recognition for doing a good job, so, they think: why waste the effort to do so?
- Resent you being their manager, mostly because they believe they're smarter than you are.

(These employees are there for a paycheck... and nothing else.)

Let me assure you of something: If you don't show your employees you care about them, appreciate them, and want to help them become more successful in their lives, you probably have a large portion of Mercenaries working for you and very few Patriots.

Pay attention here. Many of these Mercenary employees will leave you in a skinny second, and will do so for a dime more an hour offered somewhere else. There's absolutely no loyalty to you, or your company at all. If you're not the leader you should be, do you blame them? It's not their fault. It's yours!

Honestly, if you're not showing your employees you care about them and appreciate them, you don't deserve their loyalty! Do you honestly believe you can ever be successful if you have to rely on these mercenary employees to help you reach your career goals? Are these the type that make up a foundation you can build your business on? Not a chance!

Speaking of loyalty... let's look at WHY our employees aren't loyal to us today.

If you recall, in an earlier chapter, we talked about a survey done by **Gallup Research**.

During the course of surveying over 1.4 million employees, Gallup found that *"65% of American employees said they had received no recognition from their manager in the last year."*

Not once in an entire YEAR! Seriously?!!

OK, if that is really happening, and the research states that it is, then we have a real disconnect between ourselves, as managers, and our employees.

As further evidence of just how important having engaged employees is to your success, the following Gallup research, **Engagement at Work: Its Effect on Performance Continues in Tough Economic Times**, was conducted in 2012 where they examined 49,928 businesses (or work units) that included about 1.4 million employees in 192 organizations (across 49 industries and in 34 countries).

The research clearly proves that employee engagement strongly relates to key organizational outcomes in any economic climate. Even during difficult economic times, like we see today in our country and around the world, employee engagement is an important competitive differentiator for organizations.

Here are the key findings from Gallup's Q12 meta-analysis of **1.4 MILLION EMPLOYEES**:

- **Businesses that score in the top half of their organization in employee engagement have nearly double the odds of success** (based on a composite of financial, customer, retention, safety, quality, shrinkage, and absenteeism metrics) when compared with those in the bottom half. **Those at the 99th upper percentile have FOUR TIMES the success rate compared with those at the lowest percentile.**

- **Employee engagement affects NINE performance outcomes. Compared with bottom-quartile units, the upper, top-performing businesses with "Engaged Employees" have:**

- **37% lower I-don't-feel-like-going-to-work-today! excuses.**
- **25% lower turnover (in high-turnover organizations)**

- **65% lower turnover (in low-turnover organizations)**
- **28% less theft of products or inventory**
- **48% fewer safety accidents on the job**
- **41% fewer quality defects when creating your products**
- **10% higher customer satisfaction scores**
- **21% higher productivity from your employees**
- **22% higher profitability to your bottom line**

If you take a moment and add a dollar value to each of these bottom line categories that are improved by having engaged employees, it's easy to see how important it is to your success to recognize and show appreciation to your top people.

But, honestly, we really don't need research papers to tell us what we already know, do we?

Recognizing and showing appreciation to your employees is a sure-fire way to help them know how much you appreciate them and want to keep them.

Here's a perfect analogy I came up with many years ago to explain the importance of having engaged employees on our team at MyEmployees.

If you have ten engaged employees, and they're all going in the same direction, it's extremely easy to get where you want to go. Right? Yes, it is. That's what happens when you have a whole team of winners working with you and moving toward the same goal or mission.

But, let's say you have one employee (out of the ten) that doesn't want to go where you're headed, and they decide

to just sit down where they are. Now you have to drag them. With the extra weight you didn't have to deal with before, your progress really slows down. Can you imagine how hard it would be to drag this loafer along with you? It would really wear the other nine employees down, wouldn't it? This one employee is a disengaged employee. They don't care what you're doing, and will just sit there.

Alright, now let's imagine what it would be like if this disengaged employee decided to stand up again, and start pulling hard in the opposite direction from where the other nine are headed. That's what actively disengaged employees do. They make it almost impossible for the other nine to reach their goals. There's constant arguing and bickering between the two groups, and it's quite exhausting when you have to deal with this every day.

Now, do you see why you only want engaged employees on your team?

If we have any employees on our team that do not seem to be going in the right direction, we're going take action to try to get them engaged, or we'll have to fire them. Like I said earlier, "Leaders take decisive action... and losers don't!"

So, if we are to build our team with only engaged employees, we have to have buy-in from the top down. How do we get buy-in from employees at all levels of your company or department? Well, when any employee does a great job for us, and helps us reach our goals, we need to recognize him or her for that.

I often say to business managers when I speak to groups:

"EMPLOYEE RECOGNITION matters to ALL of your employees, but especially to your SUPERSTARS! These superstars are the people you most definitely want to

KEEP on your team!"

Here's a few quotes concerning the Power of Recognition from some very successful people to illustrate this:

> *"A soldier will fight long and hard for a bit of colored ribbon.*
> *Give me enough medals and I'll win you any war."*
> —Napoleon Bonaparte

> *"There are two things people want more than sex and money,*
> *and they are RECOGNITION and PRAISE."*
> —Mary Kay Ash
> Founder of Mary Kay Cosmetics

> *"Share success with the people who make it happen. It makes*
> *everybody think like an owner, which helps them build long-term*
> *relationships with customers and influences them to do things in*
> *an efficient way."*
> —Emily Ericsen, the VP of HR
> Starbucks Coffee Company

> *"Early in my career, one of the first business lessons I learned was*
> *this:*
> *It's impossible to win the hearts and minds of people unless you*
> *clearly establish goals and values and REWARD PEOPLE if they*
> *act in a way that leads to the fulfillment of those objectives. It*
> *quickly became clear to me that if you want to make sure your*
> *customers are treated well, you have to make sure you:*
> *"TREAT YOUR EMPLOYEES WELL and RECOGNIZE their*
> *efforts."*
> —F. Robert Salerno, President and COO, Avis Car Rental

Yes, my friend, as I said, employee recognition really matters to your people... and especially to your Superstars! That little piece of ribbon or that medal propels soldiers into a hail of bullets and artillery fire where they literally risk their very lives.

If you fail to see the power of that, please stop reading now. You have no business leading anyone. You may be a manager, but you are definitely not a leader. And, quite frankly, with an attitude like that, it's very unlikely you ever will be.

If you think employee recognition doesn't matter to your people, let me give you a personal example of what happens with your top people when their hard work is not appreciated.

This personal, "from the front lines" story of **David Strange** (our top salesperson I mentioned earlier in this chapter) illustrates this point very well.

Here's David with his sweet wife, Dora, and his story, in his own words...

My first real job was at a grocery store working in the Deli Department. I worked hard, and within a year I went from making $6.75/hr. to $8.00/hr. Although the pay increase was great, the work required long hours. I usually had to close the deli down every night, which meant staying late and mopping floors.

I can remember one very important, life-changing night when I was mopping and almost fainted. *I took a short break, and then tried it again. I tried several times to finish my shift, but realized something just wasn't right. The store manager happened to be closing that night, and I told him about the situation and my condition. He basically told me to suck it up and close the deli down, as there wasn't anyone else he could call in that night. I did what he asked and finished my shift.*

After getting off work and going home to bed, I began coughing, and continued coughing for hours. At 3:00 am, after feeling liquid come out with my coughs, I turned on the lights and realized I was coughing up blood. *My parents rushed me to the ER where they determined I had severe pneumonia in both lungs. They said I was lucky to be alive. I had to take the next week off to get well. I remember one of the managers calling me to find out when I would be in again, but not calling to check on my status. They were only concerned about me filling my position at work, but certainly not about me as a person. I knew at that moment I was not going to pursue a career there.*

My next job was in a sandwich shop. I took a pay cut from $8.00/hr. to $7.25, but soon realized I had made the right move. I was working for Rob, a retired Marine Corps Gunnery Sergeant. This is where I learned about work ethic. I loved working for him and the company, but there was a huge problem. I was dating my soon to be wife at the time, and knew there was no major growth opportunities working for a mom and pop's sub shop.

I applied at a Wilmington home improvement store sometime in *early 2007. At the end of the interview, when I was asked if I had any questions, I told the gentlemen that if he didn't hire me for a sales floor position, I would scrub toilets for eight hours a day if they would pay me $9/hr. I really wanted to get back to making some, what I thought was, real money. I knew it would take more than my current $7.25/hr. to feed a family. He must have liked me. When I started, they paid me $10 an hour.*

One day, after being promoted to running my own department, I just happened to be helping a gentleman who would change the course of my life. A few days later when I received a strange phone call from him, he reminded me of the great customer service I had given him and wanted to know if I was open to making a career move.

I was informed that a store manager position was opening up at the local Wilmington shoe store. I went and interviewed with the district manager. I believe I interviewed him more than he did me, and he was impressed. At the time I was making around $27,000/year at the home improvement store. I had taken the time to do the research and when we started talking money I asked for $39,000/year. I received a call later in the week for an offer of $36,000/year.

I told my store manager at the home improvement store of my decision, and he was shocked. He knew my desire to move up in the company, and insisted he would get me into the management training program within a few weeks.

Unfortunately, my decision was already made. I took the almost $10,000/yr. pay increase and went to work for the shoe store.

***Being a first-time store manager, I quickly found out that you can't train some people to greatness**. I found out that it's more important to hire the right people instead of trying to fix the wrong people. I quickly found out not everyone is trying to be the* *best they can be!*

Within eight months, my team and I had taken the store from 214/300+ stores to 4/300+ stores in year over year profit increases! My decision on whether or not to stay with the company came at the end of my first year. After having an awesome year, I was informed that due to the economy we would not be receiving bonuses. If that wasn't bad enough, the corporate office sent me a paper certificate to commemorate my achievements, and then mailed me a piece-of-junk, black plastic frame to put it in. I remember thinking to myself, "If this is all the recognition they give to their best people, my future will not be with this company."

About that time, my wife and I were praying that the Lord would open up a career move that would be better for me financially, and one that would allow me to go to church on Sundays. I happened to go to the same church as David Long's Mom and Dad. Mrs. Long had continued to encourage me, over the previous several years, to go and check out her son's company, MyEmployees.

I kept blowing her off because I wanted to become a district manager in retail one day, and frankly, I had no clue what Dave's company was all about. But, after receiving my pathetic paper certificate of achievement, I was disgusted enough to go and check them out.

During my first interview, Travis, the sales manager at the time, showed me a pay stub from a few years earlier when he started selling with the company. Never having made anywhere near that amount in annual income, much less in the first year at a company, I was, to say the least, very skeptical of a what he was telling me.

I decided to bite the bullet, and start my career with the company. I remember, during the first few training classes, Travis telling me that if something didn't improve soon, he did not think I was going to make it.

In my mind I had a choice*. I could have the right attitude about what he said to me... or I could just quit. I admit it! I sounded horrible on the phone! I was scared to death. I went home that night and practiced my sales presentation over and over again with my wife.*

The next day I came in and sounded much better. Before it was all over, I became the most successful person in my training class. I never gave up! I came to work every day with the attitude: "I will be better today than I was yesterday," something Dave always taught us to do.

I'll never forget the day I heard my manager say, "We are doing Employees of the Month presentations. Come on downstairs!"

Dave has a monthly tradition of bringing all of the (now 40+) employees together in the lobby of our company headquarters for the big presentation.

Excitement and anticipation ran through my veins as I hurried downstairs to gather with my co-workers*. Standing with everyone, I listened and watched carefully as winners were chosen from the four other departments.*

And, then I knew it was my turn...

I stood there patiently waiting until my sales manager said, "We would like to congratulate this month's 'Salesperson of the Month,' and this is his first time winning... (and then he said my name), "Mr. David Strange!"

As soon as I heard my name called out, my mind went blank from shock. I knew I had worked hard and demonstrated tremendous effort that month, but I never expected to be congratulated, much less "recognized" for it.

I will never forget the happy faces smiling at me from all of my managers and my coworkers as I walked up to receive the award. Once they handed me my plaque, every manager took the time to come over to me and shake my hand and congratulate me on winning! That was awesome!

But, it wasn't over yet. Not even close!

Dave also has another longstanding tradition of taking a picture of each winner with the management team as they receive (and then hold) their 5x7 walnut plaque in front of the other team members. Then he gives each winner their own copy of the picture of our moment in the sun, so we'll always remember our special day.

With my plaque and picture, I now had something that I could keep forever to remember my contribution to the success of the company. As the glamour shots were taken, I could hear everyone in the background clapping. Yep, it was really awesome to win!

Here's my first picture winning "Salesperson of the Month":

Another cool thing I really like is that Dave (and all five of the company managers) take all of the winners from each department to one of the fanciest restaurants in town for lunch to celebrate our success. What I ate for lunch that day escapes me now, but I do remember the dessert. I love crème brulee!

I've now won many times since that first month. It is hard to get to the top, but it is even harder to stay there. It was really awesome to win top honors six of the twelve months during my first year. I was on track to win Salesperson of the Year, and I wanted it badly!

And then it happened. I remember, very well, being in the year-end ceremony as they called out my name, "David Strange, Salesperson of the Year." I felt both proud and humbled at the same time as I accepted my beautiful 8x10 walnut plaque with my name engraved in big, gold letters. Proud, because I knew my hard work and persistence had paid off; humbled, because I knew I had now raised the bar for next year.

Consistency, hard work, and my attitude of wanting to get better and better... were the keys to winning Salesperson of the Year in my first full year with MyEmployees. I remember those months when I came in second, too. In my opinion, they were more important to me than the months I won. They motivated me. It is not how you react when you win, but when you lose, that determines your success. What will you do then?

But that is not the end of my "story."

There were more changes happening in my life that I wasn't even aware of. The company had weekly Book Club meetings. Not only was I making far more money than I ever had before (over three times more, in fact), but I was learning how to improve my life... both inside and outside of work. In our weekly meetings we were

164

reading books I had never heard of before, such as, **How to Win Friends and Influence People, by Dale Carnegie**, and **The 12 Essential Rules of Becoming Indispensable, by Dr. Tony Zeiss.**

We were also watching Dave Ramsey videos on how to get out of debt and build financial security, among countless others to develop our leadership skills. We learned how to set goals, and better yet, how to accomplish them.

Speaking of goals, as I am typing this, I can tell you that by the end of this year my family and I will be debt free (other than our house payment). We are now living on a budget, and have thousands of dollars in our savings account! More importantly, I have been attending church more regularly, and have been able to grow spiritually as well.

In recognition of my hard work, Dave also purchased Dora and me a membership at our local Gold's Gym. After a year, or so, of working out and losing weight, we are now off of cholesterol medication, and I personally have lost ten pounds and six inches off my waist.

I love the fact that, in my career with MyEmployees, I get to help my client companies build programs to recognize the contributions of thousands of their employees each year. I love to come to work every day, and I get great satisfaction in knowing what I do affects so many people, and in such powerful ways. I'm changing lives for the better!

Dave always tells each of us to "treat our position within the company as if it's our own small business within our business." Every day, we get out what we put in. Our company, MyEmployees, gives me the tools and training to do my job. I just need to show up and take advantage of the opportunities. **Another thing Dave always says is, "You are either** *getting better, or you are getting worse. There is no staying the same."*

Working for Dave has taught me so much over these four years, both inside and outside of work. I realize now that all my career moves in the past have helped me get ready for the real career opportunity I have now!

I'll end by briefly describing my growing relationship with Dave. I think one person's description of him pretty much sums it up. He told me, "David Long is more than a leader. He is a people trainer who helps his people get the most out of their lives." Zig Ziglar once said (and this is one of Dave's favorite quotes), **"You can get everything in life you want if you will just help enough other people get what they want."** *This is a testament to the caliber of man David Long is. He has a relentless passion to help improve everyone (and everything) in the company.*

Dave has gotten to where he is today by following this simple principle. *He has helped thousands of people get more out of life than they had ever hoped (including me!), and in return he has been immensely blessed. I can honestly say, without hesitation, that Dave truly cares about every one of his employees. I also know that he wants more for them, sometimes, than they want for themselves. Our company will continue to grow, improve, and prosper because of his love and concern for each of us.*

When you teach others around you how to reach their true potential, they can then add more value to your own life and business. *When you do this out of true love and compassion (as Dave does), people realize it, give you their loyalty, and are more than willing to help you achieve your goals. This is what has happened in my life, and for that I am eternally grateful!*

Thanks, **David Strange**
Employee Engagement Expert

I greatly appreciate David's kind words about me and the company culture I've strived to create. He is one of our best, and I want to take a moment and analyze (as we did with Adam and Yuichi) some key points that he brought out in his story. Please don't miss them.

Key Points from David's Story:

1. **He wasn't recognized at all by his manager in the grocery store**. Hmmm... Adam said the same thing about his first job at the grocery store. Apparently, there is real opportunity within the industry to set yourself apart as a manager IF you happen to work in that industry.

If it wasn't bad enough that he didn't get noticed, even when he was near death, the manager only cared about David showing up to do his job, but showed no concern at all that he had to go into the hospital.

2. **When David was recognized in the shoe business for his great accomplishment in improving the store ranking within the company, they did not make a huge deal about it.** They just mailed him a "paper certificate and a cheap plastic frame," as David said. Sadly, that reminds me of some of the horror stories I've heard from employees down through the years. Some say they received paper certificates and were told they "needed to buy their own frame"! How foolish some managers are. As the old phrase goes, they were "penny wise and pound (the British dollar) foolish!" They blew the chance to show their appreciation with a cheap (very cheap, actually) gesture.

3. **From David's own words, you realize he has experienced real "life changes" by being in an environment where he is appreciated (and recognized) for his great accomplishments, but more**

167

importantly... where he is growing as a person.

Please don't underestimate the power of helping your people "grow" toward their goals. They will give you their loyalty and their hearts if you do.

Feb 2014 – Update on David Strange: Hard work and consistency have paid off, and as a result, I'm very proud to say he has been promoted to manage our Recognition Consultants as the new "RC" Manager.

Congratulations, David! It's well deserved, son!

I can't begin to count the managers I've heard down through the years who say crazy things like, "I don't have any of my 50 employees that deserve to be recognized!"

What? Are you kidding me?!!

Let me clear up something for you right now, and anyone whoever says something ignorant like this. If you don't have someone (not one, but many employees... if you have 50) that deserves to be recognized for doing a great job that month, look in the mirror, my friend! There's the problem! Your people deserve better, so be better!

When we hear a manager tell us "no employee deserves recognition this month," it's just a matter of time before that manager is replaced. It never fails. Any manager who has that me-against-them attitude toward their employees will receive a nice little visit from the district manager, where he or she will be sure to ask for their keys.

Statistics, such as the research I shared with you from the Gallup organization, prove how important recognition is to everyone!

Yes, it is a very, VERY BIG Deal!

All right, we now understand that our employees constantly crave recognition and showing them that they matter, so let's move on and learn how to amplify our successful results.

And now, let's move on to the **D** in our

Management R.E.W.A.R.D.S. Principles.

Chapter 8

DUPLICATION

"Treat people as if they were what they ought to be,
and you help them to become what they are capable of
being."
—Johann Wolfgang von Goethe

My sweet wife, Janet, is a big ancestry.com freak, and has spent a few years researching both of our family trees all the way back to the 1500s. Yes, ol' Dave here has some pretty famous relatives.

Sir Robert Bell (1539-1577) was Speaker of the House of Commons of Great Britain, and was also knighted during the reign of Queen Elizabeth I.

Another relative was 2nd Major Malachi Bell, who fought in the Revolutionary War, and was a member of the North Carolina Constitutional Convention in 1789. He represented Eastern North Carolina in ratifying the new US Constitution, too.

Anyway, as I was saying before, I chase my proverbial ancestral rabbits, while Janet spends many hours on the ancestry.com website and is always looking to see what the newest little "leaf" will show her. A leaf is a little icon that appears, occasionally, when you log onto the website, telling you that someone else has posted some information that may relate to your family tree. She loves the thrill of potentially finding, and then adding, more lost relatives to her, or my, ever-growing ancestral family tree charts.

"OK, Dave, that's a great story about your dead relatives, but how does that apply to me as a manager?"

Good question. Here's why it matters...

As a manager who is developing his/her career, you, in essence, should always be concerned about creating your own management family tree by hiring, grooming, then sending out other successful managers to continue the growth of the company. These successful managers of your lineage are essentially your management offspring.

Before we go any further, let me ask you this:

"Do YOU have aspirations of becoming a district manager, or higher, in your company?"

If so, what are you doing now to make that a reality? One thing is certain. You will not get there by accident. There has to be a plan, and it must be followed until your goal is reached. I'm going to do everything within my power to help make that a reality for you.

One saying comes to mind for me here...

"The lead dog always has the best view. The only view the other dogs ever see is the butt of the dog(s) in front of them!"

So, how do we begin to improve your standings in the company rankings?

That's quite simple really. Start with where you are right NOW.

Grab the list of things your district manager said you needed to fix/improve the last time they visited your business. That's the best place to start. How many of them have you fixed already? Did you tell them when the tasks were completed? If not, don't assume they know.

Now, if they came to your store, and didn't tell you to fix something, they probably won't be a district manager too much longer. It's the manager's job (at any level) to tell those within their team how to fix or improve various aspects of their business to make them more successful. If any manager fails to do that, what good are they? Not much!

One thing I always did when I started a new position within a company (regardless of the position) was to find out who the top person or manager was, and then ask them out to lunch. Then I picked their brain on how I could become as successful as they were. It never failed. I have had several people tell me they could talk for a few minutes, but I never had one spend less than two hours with me... EVER!

That's the beautiful thing about wanting to be the best at something. When you ask a successful person HOW they became successful, they'll always take the time to tell you. I've never seen an exception to this.

For the price of a steak, or sandwich, you can get the career advice from the best, most successful people in your company. These folks have been-there-done-that better than anyone else! There simply is no better source for the knowledge you'll need to reach the next level.

"Successful people are always looking for opportunities to help others. Unsuccessful people are always asking, 'What's in it for me?'"
—Brian Tracy, Success Guru

Small-minded people only care about themselves, and are extremely selfish. Perhaps you've worked for someone like that. I know I have. The good news is, for us anyway, that they normally don't stay in management positions very long.

Another source for knowledge is reading books, or attending seminars. You must constantly be feeding your mind and expanding your knowledge base. Few people will take the time to do either. That will set you apart from the rest.

I remember one time the area representative for the Dale Carnegie Course came to our district manager's meeting and gave a presentation. Our district manager said the company would pay for half the course fee if any of us wanted to attend the course. Out of the 42 managers present, I was the only one who ended up accepting the offer. Not one other manager was willing to spend $250 to increase their chances for success.

Not one!

Interestingly enough, during the Carnegie presentation, hardly anyone said anything when the representative asked questions... so I answered him more than most. Immediately after the presentation, my district manager pulled me aside and told me I needed to go apologize because I "harassed the speaker" (his exact words). So, I went to the representative and asked for his forgiveness. He was shocked. "Are you kidding me?" he said. "You were the only one in that group with a pulse!"

Did I mention that my district manager was replaced a few months later? No? Hmmm... Go figure.

This is a great time to show what I believe sums up the difference between successful people and the rest. This is exactly, word for word, what I teach my team.

Here it is:

"Successful people DO what unsuccessful people AREN'T WILLING TO DO... even though they don't want to do it either. They just DO IT!"

Does that describe you? If not, more than likely you won't ever become a Top 10% Manager. Take the action needed to succeed. It's so much better being at the top of the list!

Note: for the next illustration I have for you, we will use a retail store manager as our example, but the same principles apply regardless of the industry.

I'm sure, if you're a company store manager, you receive several monthly financial spreadsheets (such as your P&L, etc.) showing how you're doing on sales, profits, etc. There are many books available that can help you better understand them, so we won't waste time on them here.

But, I DO want to talk about the tracking form that shows you where you and your store stand within the rankings of your district. This form will probably show you at least five to ten critical financial numbers that describe where you fall within the rankings. Your place on the list today will be your "starting point"!

So, where do you stand in the district rankings?

Near the top... or closer to the bottom?

As a former retail manager myself, for over five years, I always looked forward to those reports because I had the attitude (and goal) of climbing higher and higher each month.

Let me share a little-known secret I learned when I was in my 20s. It has served me well through the years.

Here it is:

The FIRST THING your company's upper-level managers will check, when determining if YOU should become the newest member of their team, is your "genealogical management chart." They want to see who you hired, trained, helped get promoted, and how they've fared once they were managing their own company location.

And, now for another "slap upside the head" moment...

Fact: If you've been a manager in your present company for many years, you should have quite the genealogical chart of successful managers, trained by you, who are currently serving in management positions in other company locations.

If you don't have many (or any) superstar managers out there that you've personally trained, we definitely have some work to do.

Pay careful attention here: If you fail in your ability to reproduce other great managers through your efforts, then your career will soon come to a screeching halt, if it hasn't already.

Now, before you start to stress out and order some Viagra for your rather "impotent and less than vigorous lineage," just put your mind at ease for a moment. This is not something you have to fix alone. In fact, I believe that's the best part about this.

If you've been following my advice in the earlier chapters, and have begun to implement each strategy, you're already well on your way to rectifying your inadequacies in this very important area of your strategic career development.

At this point you may want to say, *"Dave, I have been a manager for two years, and I don't have any managers that I have helped get promoted. What do I need to do?"*

OK, let's start with the basics.

I want you to think of each of these current superstar members of your team as "mini-me's." (Yes, just like in the Austin Power's movie... only they're probably a little taller). If you are truly one of the best your company has in management, then it is your responsibility to create more successful managers just like yourself. As I said just a few paragraphs earlier, that is the number one factor your company's upper management team looks for in the process of promoting anyone to the next level in their career.

By now you should have determined who your best people are in each department in your business and personally started to groom them.

By the way, sometimes the best team members in a particular department do not include the current manager.

Fix that immediately. If you're tolerating incompetence, especially within your management team, your credibility within the entire business is in jeopardy.

Like I said, "Fix it now!"

Now let's take a moment to look at my...

Shark's Teeth Strategy of Leadership Development.

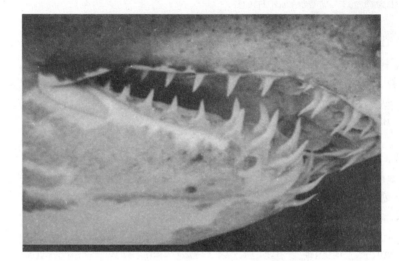

Having grown up on the beaches of the North Carolina coast, and learning to surf as a teenager, I'm pretty familiar with sharks. Sometimes, a little too familiar.

Let's just say that I've seen a few of them up close and personal during my younger days. In fact, I actually petted one (purely by accident, I assure you) on the only day I ever skipped school... but that's a story for another time.

If you know anything about sharks, you know they have a set of teeth like no other creature on earth. In fact, it's more like an assembly line with each front tooth having three or four other teeth behind it... just waiting for their opportunity to move up to the front row.

Notice the multiple smaller teeth behind the front teeth in the shark's mouth. If a tooth falls out, or is pulled out during an attack on its prey, another pops up to take its place.

That is exactly what you need to think about as you develop your leadership team. Occasionally, for whatever reason, a manager either gets promoted (hopefully), leaves, or gets fired.

Hey, it happens. Just like the shark's teeth, you need to have another leader in reserve, ready to pop into place when their opportunity arises.

All the current leaders in your business represent the front row of the shark's teeth.

One practice that I have kept for years is to ask my managers:

"If something happened to you, who would you recommend to take your place, and why?"

Once that person is named, and the manager explains why they've chosen this individual, the real discussion begins. The other managers get to voice their opinion of the newly mentioned management candidate, and how they feel about them. Are there any issues the other managers know about this individual that may have slipped their manager's attention? If so, we discuss it.

If we are all in agreement, this candidate is asked to start reading books, watching DVDs, and listening to CDs on leadership development. If they do so, the manager starts incorporating them into the decisions that affect their department. Perhaps they are given some reports to keep up with every day. Maybe they will help train a new employee.

In essence, they take on an assistant manager role... without the title.

If they balk at doing any of the above mentioned tasks we ask them to do (all required for the manager's job)... we move on to another "tooth." This candidate will not be a good choice to join our management team.

OK, once you've got a solid management team in place and you've incorporated my **Shark's Teeth Strategy of Leadership Development**, lining up your future leaders, you're ready to start working on my:

3-Step Strategy to Get Your Superstars Promoted.

STEP 1: Sit down with each member of your management team, and ask about their dreams and aspirations for their future with the company. Do they want to be promoted to manage their own business? You'll be surprised when you find some don't, and that's OK. Not everyone has the desire or ambition to run their own business. All you need to do is have their commitment to help others along the way who do have higher career aspirations in life.

If you find that a particular manager is not on board with your employee development program, or stands in the way of it happening in their department, attempt to get them onboard, and replace them immediately if they don't get in line. They will sabotage your efforts.

STEP 2: Assess who the best people are within each department. Have each manager write down who they feel are the five "best" employees in their department. Once you have their list, have them tell you, in detail, WHY they feel these folks are the best. Do they feel each of these people are "management material"? This is an exercise to determine whether or not they understand the attributes of a real winner, and what a superstar employee looks/sounds/acts like. These are your foundational employees for the next generation of managers you will groom and develop, so we definitely need to make sure we're starting off with the right people. If they are weak, your chances of success will be greatly diminished.

Think of it like this: You are the tree trunk with very deep roots; the stable base from which everyone else will grow.

Your current management team represents the main branches, and you must trust them to hire/prune/train their best employees (the smaller branches), because this is your feeder program for future management development.

You need to make sure all your best people are on board and loyal to you. That starts with your loyalty to them. Remember my analogy of the fireplace: Firewood first, heat later.

One powerful, easy-to-implement habit I started a few years ago to increase the loyalty between my people and me is this:

Find FIVE people in your business that you can brag on EVERY day!

Yes, I know we've already discussed how powerful employee recognition is, so I won't cover that again here, but you need to realize it's not an option if you want to be immensely successful. This practice takes your bond with your superstars to another level! It's the most powerful weapon in your management arsenal, so use it, and use it OFTEN!

Here's my **"Find FIVE a Day" strategy** I do every day, with rare exceptions, unless I'm on vacation, or something similar:

I look at the sales charts (and other charts on my management dashboard), and decide which five superstars get my attention for the day. I go visit them if I'm in the office, spend some time bragging on them for a specific accomplishment I noticed, shake their hand, and tell them how proud I am of them.

If I'm traveling, or not in the office that day, I send them a text, a card, or an email letting them know that I'm watching over them, I'm proud of them, and I want to help them be more successful with us.

I constantly vary the delivery method so they don't get used to hearing from me in only one way. I want them to know I'm always overseeing their commitment to excellence in their job, their progress, and their results for the company.

By the way, we just created our own Spot-On Cards Recognition Program featuring small, handwritten cards for these everyday recognition moments. Obviously, they are not going to be as powerful as the monthly recognition where we honor them publicly in front of all employees with walnut engraved plaques, but don't underestimate the power of a handwritten note.

Here's a picture of some of the cards:

Here's a link to see the card package, if you're interested:

www.MyEmployees.com/Cards

OK, here's the final piece of my **3-Step Strategy to Get Your Superstars Promoted**.

STEP 3: Once the magic starts to happen, become a true campaign manager for the members of your management team. You should be constantly looking for ways to shamelessly promote your best managers to your district manager and regional manager. This is very critical. At every opportunity, you'll want to talk up the top managers on your management team to your boss(es).

Let me expand on that one a little more, so you'll fully understand what we're after. It is very common for this principle to trip up insecure, fearful managers, causing them to ignore this important aspect of their own career development.

It would amaze you, but **there are many managers who are afraid to brag on someone else (even one of their own managers) because they feel it will make them appear weak**. That's ridiculous, but managers sometimes feel that way.

If anything, talking about the virtues and accomplishments of one of your managers only makes you look great. It shows upper management that you're not some weak, pathetic, jealous loser who is afraid to shine the light on someone else. That's what true leadership is.

Here's something else to think about:

Members of upper management, just like you, are busy doing their jobs, and will probably not see every great and amazing thing you or your managers do, unless you bring it to their attention. If you are always looking for ways to make your managers look good, this obviously creates massive loyalty between them and you.

Keep in mind, this only makes you look good to upper management too, because the manager you're speaking about is one of yours, and his successes are a direct reflection on your management strengths.

Bragging on your people accomplishes two things, both of which are vital to your success, and to the success of your team.

> **1. It shows management that you are developing your team**. This is huge when a regional manager starts looking for a new district manager to add to their team. They're going to want someone who is a proven builder of people, and someone who gets the job done themselves.

> **2. It shows management that you are a strong source for developing the future leaders who will be needed in the district**. Do everything you can to help your people look great to your district manager, because it helps all of you look highly competent as leaders.

All right, let's change gears here, and elaborate more on how to groom our best people for management...

As I've already told you, my Book Club meetings accomplish many things for us. One thing they help do is show us who our leaders are. True leaders will always speak up and step forward when asked for their contributions. I've rarely seen a quiet person get noticed in my lifetime. That's one of the reasons I started the Book Clubs in the beginning. I saw some great qualities in some of my people, but they were not assertive in any way. I wanted to give them an opportunity to show others what I saw in them. Thankfully, that has happened many times for us.

Once you've assessed who your best people are in each department, you need to personally spend some extra time with them, beyond just seeing them at a Book Club meeting. These are your superstars. Treat them as such.

You'll need to spend some money on leadership training. If you have not already done so, start to build your own library. As I've said, my personal library is easily worth over $300,000 and it's growing more every day!

For management training (for yourself and your team) I highly recommend John Maxwell's books and DVD courses. We've used his books and courses extensively in our company, and he's quite thorough in his teaching. I have no affiliation with them, but maybe I should.

Here's the link: http://www.johnmaxwell.com/

"The greatest good you can do for another is not just share your riches but to reveal to him, his own."
—Benjamin Disraeli

Remember, your people are a direct reflection of you as their leader. Make them something you want the world (and definitely upper management) to see. Leave nothing to chance.

"You were born to win, but to be a winner, you must plan to win, prepare to win, and expect to win."
—Zig Ziglar, Motivational Speaker

Final thought: As I said earlier, "You will not become successful by accident." It must be planned for, and acted upon.

What action will you take today to get started on your plans for enhancing your career success, and the success of your people?

And that brings us to **S**, the final letter, in our

Management R.E.W.A.R.D.S. Principles.

Chapter 9

SUCCESS

(Focusing on the things that matter most)

"Every man dies, but not every man truly lives."
—William Wallace

What does "success" mean to you?

Dictionary.com defines success as, "The attainment of wealth, position, honors, or the like. A performance or achievement that is marked by success, as by the attainment of honors."

However, if we went around asking people, I doubt very seriously that any two people would define it the same way.

One person might consider living on a quiet farm in Idaho the epitome of his success, but someone else might call that an absolute nightmare.

Another may think that success means retiring to a beach hut at 30, while someone else would say, "Heck no! I will know I've been successful when I'm still a music mogul at 85!" As they say, "It takes all kinds to make a world."

So, let's talk a little now about what you feel will make you successful.

The vast majority of individuals in the world would probably agree that if they had a lot of money, they would consider themselves successful.

Turn on the TV and look at the reality shows like *Survivor, The Biggest Loser, Big Brother,* and *American Idol*. What is the Grand Prize they are trying to win? Usually, it's perceived as a very large amount of money.

During the final weigh-in, or final performance, the victor is chosen. We see them raise their fists in jubilation before the enthusiastic, cheering crowd. Sound familiar?

As it says in the Bible, Ecclesiastes 1:9, "There is nothing new under the sun." People have been striving for money for eons.

So, if all of these TV shows have money as the goal, I guess it's safe to say, **Having lots of money must be the end goal if you're to be considered successful.**

A little personal note here: I've been immensely blessed, financially, in my lifetime. God has given me, as I shared Dave Ramsey's quote earlier, "Much more than I deserve." And I have to say, the vast majority of people I know who find themselves in a similar situation—successful, with a lot of money—are the most generous people I've ever met.

The image of Ebenezer Scrooge sitting in a dark room, counting his golden guineas is anything but reality. Honestly, I have to laugh at the media's portrayal of the wealthy today. The media's mission to vilify anyone who works hard and insinuate that they are wealthy because they stole the money from someone else is ludicrous!

Yes, there are people out there like Bernie Madoff, who stole many millions of dollars from his investors, but he's not the norm. If you believe that all people who have money are evil, then you'll never be wealthy.

Here's the simple prescription for becoming successful in the world today, regardless of what you do for a career:

Deliver VALUE people are willing to PAY for.

It's as simple as that.

Someone once said, "You don't have a customer until someone buys from you a second time. The first time they buy from you, you made a sale. However, if you don't deliver the value they thought they were paying for, they won't come back again."

Speaking of customer service...

My friend and mentor, Jeffrey Gitomer, has written an excellent book on delivering the type of customer service that will have your clients saying, "Heck yeah, I'll buy from you again!" when you ask them to repurchase your products or services. It's an excellent choice to teach your staff how to truly take care of your clients or customers. In fact, we've used this book to train our own staff.

His great book is titled: ***Customer Satisfaction is Worthless, Customer Loyalty is Priceless: How to Make Them Love You, Keep You Coming Back, and Tell Everyone They Know***.

On Jeffrey's website, www.Gitomer.com, you'll also find a vast assortment of books, DVDs, and anything related to being better at sales and/or taking excellent care of your clients and customers. It would be a good idea to know this information, so you can teach it to your employees.

OK, let's get back to talking about success and money.

Here's a principle that I hope you will take to heart, because it is so true.

Money Does NOT Buy Happiness!

If you equate success with money, and money with happiness, you are setting yourself up for a world of hurt.

Yes, I know you're probably saying, *"Yeah, Dave, well I'm willing to find out if you give me some of it!"*

To that I would say, *"Be careful what you wish for!"*

Perhaps you saw the news story about the largest lottery winning jackpot of all time (at that time) on ABC's "20/20" news magazine program. I found another article about it on BusinessWeek.com by author David Samuels (I've summarized what he wrote to keep it brief, only sharing the pertinent points of the story).

Here's the story...

"Lottery Winner Jack Whittaker's Losing Ticket"

Jack Whittaker, a 55 year old contractor from Scott Depot, West Virginia, had worked his way up from backcountry poverty to build a water and sewer pipe business that employed over 100 people. He was a millionaire several times over. But, when he awoke at 5:45 a.m. on Christmas morning in 2002, everything he'd built in his life held only passing significance next to a scrap of paper in his worn leather wallet—a $1 Powerball lottery ticket.

On Christmas Eve, when he bought the ticket, the prize stood at $280 million. A late surge of buyers pushed it to $314.9 million, making Whittaker the winner of the biggest single undivided jackpot in lottery history (at that time).

There was something about Whittaker's lottery winnings that felt different from the money he'd earned as a businessman. "I've had to work for everything in my life," he said at that first press conference. **"This is the first thing that's ever been given to me."**

There is no shortage of lottery winners who go broke—enough to fill many seasons of reality television—but there was good reason to think that Whittaker, a successful businessman whose journey from rags to riches was the product of self-reliance and hard work, would make good use of his new wealth.

The idea that 10 years later he would wish he'd torn up his winning ticket and thrown away the pieces would have struck him and everyone who knew him as nuts.

Whittaker's faith that he could handle his enormous lottery winnings with the same qualities of self-reliance, hard work, and aggression that had allowed him to master previous challenges was tragically misplaced.

Months later, he was arrested after driving his Hummer into a concrete median on the West Virginia Turnpike.

His transformation from successful businessman and loving

grandfather to disheveled and obnoxious strip club patron took less than two years, and alienated many of his friends and family members, beginning with his wife, Jewel, who soon filed for divorce.

Most lottery winners suffer tremendous guilt as the result of their good fortune; they're also troubled by family members and friends who feel entitled to their winnings and who become angry when they don't get what they feel they deserve.

Without access to financially and psychologically sophisticated advice, winners quickly find themselves easy marks for every kind of manipulation and often take refuge in pre-existing addictions, which are compounded by seemingly inexhaustible wealth.

It was Whittaker's dream that Brandi Bragg, his 15 year old granddaughter, would inherit everything he had amassed; he planned to give all of his companies and associated properties to her when she turned 21.

"She was the shining star of my life, and she was what it was all about for me," he later said. "From the day she was born, it was all about providing and protecting and taking care of her."

Whittaker lavished her with money and gifts, including the pale-blue custom-painted Mitsubishi she had wanted and at least four other cars. According to her friends, it wasn't unusual for him to hand Bragg $5,000 in cash to spend in a single day, which didn't bring her happiness, but an entourage of drug dealers and petty criminals.

Within a year of Whittaker's windfall, Bragg went into rehab for Oxycontin addiction, but she quickly relapsed. "They want her for her money and not for her good personality," Whittaker complained a year after his win to

a reporter from the Associated Press. "She's the most bitter 16 year old I know."

Surrounded by enablers and local kids who wanted to share in her wealth, Bragg dropped out of school and spent her days sleeping and shopping, and her nights driving aimlessly and buying large quantities of junk food to keep her entourage fed. She also smoked "a lot of crack. Big rocks of crack," according to J.C. Shaver, one of the men who broke into Whittaker's house in September 2004.

According to a reporter who peeked inside, the interior of Bragg's Mitsubishi was littered with candy wrappers, soda bottles, DVDs, and loose 5, 10, and 20 dollar bills—the change from the stacks of hundreds Whittaker gave her as spending money. Hundred dollar bills would fly around inside the car and sometimes out the window as she cruised around with friends, one of them recalled. "She doesn't want to be in charge of the money. She doesn't want to inherit the money. She just looks for her next drugs," Whittaker told a reporter in 2004.

He had plenty of problems of his own. At one point, Whittaker estimated that he'd been involved in 460 illegal actions since winning the lottery – an estimate quickly superseded by further arrests, along with more lawsuits, some of which were thinly veiled attempts at extortion.

His attempts to recover money he'd loaned to friends and acquaintances were often expensive and usually in vain. In the hope of keeping trouble away, Whittaker hired off-duty sheriff's deputies to guard his house and serve as bodyguards.

On December 20th, a girl's body was found wrapped in a plastic tarp behind a junked van in Scary Creek, an unincorporated area outside the town of St. Albans. The girl's body was in bad enough shape that police needed to use tattoos on the corpse to formally identify her as

Brandi Bragg, Whittaker's granddaughter.

Bragg had pills and a syringe hidden in her bra and cocaine and methadone in her system at the time of her death, which was ruled to be the result of an accidental overdose.

Things didn't get much better for Whittaker after Bragg's death. In April 2008, his divorce from Jewel was finalized, ending nearly 42 years of marriage. In July of the following year, his daughter Ginger Whittaker Bragg was found dead in her opulent home on Lake Drive in Daniels. She was 42 years old.

In the end, after losing family and friends, Jack Whittaker said,

"I wish I'd torn that ticket up!"

To me, that was a truly sad story of someone who, by the world's standards, got what we all dream of by winning the lottery. But, in the end, it destroyed his life!

Now, lest you be so arrogant as to say, "That guy couldn't handle the money! I wouldn't have done all of those stupid things he did with it!" remember this. Mr. Whittaker was already a successful, multi-millionaire BEFORE he won the huge, multi-million dollar lottery.

He was already accustomed to having money, just not that much of it. If you've never had millions of your own, it's highly unlikely that you would fare any better if you were to have won that lottery jackpot yourself.

Not to quote Scripture all the time, but the Bible says,

"The LOVE of money is the root of all evil."

Pay attention here!

Money is not evil. Money is nothing more than a tool.

It is neither good, nor bad. The same money can buy food for the hungry, or it can buy drugs for the addict. It can buy a home for a family, or it can buy a bomb to destroy it.

Here's something else about money you should know.

Money is an Amplifier of the REAL YOU.

If you're an evil person, who only cares about yourself, then acquiring more money will only increase your selfish, destructive nature. In addition to that, you'll become paranoid to the point where you think others are constantly trying to steal your money away from you.

If I asked you to name a movie where someone got a lot of money that ended up wreaking havoc on his life, what movie would you name?" I'm sure I'm not alone in choosing *Scarface* with Al Pacino playing the role of Tony Montana, a Cuban immigrant who became involved in the drug trade in Miami.

Here's a photo showing Tony (near the end of the movie) as he's sitting at his desk piled high with cocaine only minutes before his lavish estate is overrun by a rival drug cartel gang. Just by looking at him here you can see how empty he must feel inside.

Does he look happy to you? Not a chance! In fact, during a drug-fueled tirade a few minutes earlier, Tony had killed his best friend because he was romantically involved with his sister. Their romance had been going on behind Tony's back for months, and they had secretly married a few weeks earlier. Tony obviously did not approve.

If there was anything good inside of him, it had long since died.

On the other hand, if you're a kind person who truly cares about others, money will amplify the goodness within you, enabling you to be an even more generous person.

"So, Dave, if I shouldn't be focused on making money and using that alone to define my success, what am I supposed to be aiming for in my life?" Good question.

I don't know if you're familiar with TED Talks, but it's a huge database of mostly short videos from experts in various fields. There's one by Richard St. John, a man who had it all... and then lost most of it.

St. John had what the world would consider success, but squandered it away. St. John started to focus more on the money he was making, and less on the clients that supplied it to his business. He explains how "success is a journey, and not a destination" in his TED Talk, sharing his personal experiences. The video is approximately six minutes long, and well worth your time. Enjoy.

You can see his video @ www.MyEmployees.com/Resources
Click on the link: TED Video.

As I said earlier, my late father, Rev. Dr. J.W. Long, was a Baptist preacher. Upon my graduation from high school, my parents gave me a new, leather-bound Bible, and inside was this handwritten inscription:

"Remember, son, success is finding the Will of God for your life... and doing it!"

My father was right. It's as simple as that! It's true I'm wealthy by the world's standards. But that's not why I'm successful. Not even close! It's because I get up early every day, and look forward to doing what I love! I do not allow the financial success I've earned to distract me from my mission.

I have a company that is changing people's lives every single day! How many people can say that? I'm not just talking about our clients either. I'm talking about my own people too, my employees. That's what I love. Not the financial gain. It's nothing more than a way to keep score, as someone once said, but it should never be the goal.

I love this quote:

"Love what you do, and you'll never work a day in your life."

Yes, I know. You've heard that too, and some might even say that work is a four-letter word. But, if you can get yourself to the place where you really like your work, it will no longer be something you want to avoid.

Listen! If you get up every day, and you literally dread going to work, set about changing that right now. Life is too short to do otherwise. And speaking of a too-short life: It's been proven that the number one day for heart attacks, by a large margin, is Monday. More specifically, it's Monday morning.

Why do you suppose that is?

It's because millions of people can't imagine another day of going to a workplace they despise. They dread it so much it makes them physically ill.

I pray that cannot be said of you.

Personally, here's how I made my work a "game." I always used to compete against myself just to see if I could beat last year's sales numbers by 20%. Sometimes, this is not easy to do, especially as the company grows. This strategy keeps you focused on the end results, and helps you minimize the mundane daily tasks that trip up most people, and cause them to hate their jobs.

Over the years, I've read many books about being happy at work, and there are three main ingredients that people feel need to be included for them to find a career opportunity they will love!

If you want to be happy at work, here are the three main things you should look for:

> **1: Have many friends at work. It's been proven, over and over again, if you have friends on the job, your satisfaction at work is greatly enhanced.** Do you have a lot of friends on the job? If you do, statistically speaking, you're going to be happy to see them every day. If not, you'll more than likely be miserable. Remember, "To have friends, you must be a friend."
>
> This is certainly one of the things we look for when we hire people. We want happy, personable employees so that our clients (and our employees) will enjoy interacting with them.
>
> **2: Opportunity for career advancement. Make sure you have opportunities to grow into new positions as**

the company continues to grow and expand. One key point I share with my employees is this: If you aren't prepared when opportunity comes, you'll be like two ships passing in the night, and the opportunity will pass by you and on to someone else.

Remember, preparation must come first, and is required for you to be ready when opportunity comes your way. Nobody controls that better than the individuals themselves. Take the proper initiative to make sure you're preparing yourself for the day you see your opportunity ship approaching.

3: Opportunity for personal growth. You need to be in an environment where you are consciously focusing on getting better in all aspects of your life. As a manager, you have many hats to wear. You have to have many skills, and you'll be using them quite often.

Sometimes you need to be a great public speaker that has to rally the troops toward reaching, and then beating, a certain sales goal your corporate office has set for you.

Maybe you've recently had an employee who has lost a relative, and you need to be there to help console them in their hour of need by just letting them know you care.

Sadly, sometimes you need to be able to decide disputes between employees, or even department managers.

Do you have those skills? If not, you must keep learning, so you know how to handle these situations.

You must constantly be learning new things that will help you advance and be a better manager. This is your journey of success. Does your company have ongoing programs that are designed to help you get better, or are you just expected to do your job?

If they don't, and that's the case in many companies, it's your responsibility to take charge of your continuing education. Trust me. It will pay off for you with higher income and promotions.

> *"Formal education will make you a living;*
> *SELF-EDUCATION will make you a FORTUNE."*
> —Jim Rohn

If you've tried to do everything I've shared with you, and you're still not happy on your job, you might consider reading a book titled, ***What Color is Your Parachute?***

Look for the link to the book @
www.Top10Manager.com/Resources

Click on the *"What Color is Your Parachute?"* Book

This book has been reprinted many times, and it's because it helps people decide what career or type of job would be best for them by asking a series of questions. Like I said, "If you're unhappy, do something about it!"

Do you honestly think you can ever be truly successful unless you're doing something with your life that makes you happy?

Not a chance!

Now, if you do love your career, then give it your all! Become the employee that you would want working for you. Become the manager you would want to work for. Set the example for others to follow.

Here's how your attitude should be toward your employer. This quote was written many years ago, but the wisdom is timeless.

Check it out...

"If you work for a man, in heaven's name work for him. If he pays you wages which supply you bread and butter, work for him; speak well of him; stand by him, and stand by the institution he represents. If put to a pinch, an ounce of loyalty is worth a pound of cleverness.

If you must vilify, condemn, and eternally disparage, resign your position, and when you are outside, damn to your heart's content, but as long as you are part of the institution do not condemn it. If you do that, you are loosening the tendrils that are holding you to the institution, and at the first high wind that comes along, you will be uprooted and blown away, and will probably never know the reason why."
—Elbert Hubbard, American Author

That being said, if you don't believe you can give your all to the company you work for, then find one for which you can. But, first of all, make sure the problem is not with you (which it is many times) before you abandon your current position.

Here's something to think about: You've worked hard to be promoted to management where you are currently. If you go somewhere else you'll probably have to start again at the bottom. Isn't it easier to adjust your attitude, and recommit to being the best manager you can be right where you are now? Yes, it is.

Besides, if you implement the ideas I've shared with you in this book, you should see a radical change in your life in only a few months, if not sooner.

But, there will be challenges wherever you go, and with any company you work for. Do not let them affect your attitude. You have complete control over that yourself. If you allow your attitude to slip, there will be consequences. They usually end with you working somewhere else, so don't be foolish.

As a real world example, here's the story of one of my own employees who started taking for granted how good she had it.

If you recall, I've added a few stories of some of the best MyEmployees employees at our company in some of the other chapters. Well, here's an email I received from an employee we had to let go, regrettably, over a year ago.

A little background on her first: She was our highest paid salesperson at the time, so there were real financial ramifications from letting her go.

But, as managers, we always have to look at the big picture and make our decisions based on the best interests of all of our employees as a whole. Not just one.

Sadly, she allowed personal problems to affect her work life.

We sincerely tried to help her get past them (by sitting her down and letting her know there was a problem), but her attitude continued to deteriorate to where she was constantly attacking her fellow employees.

As I said, we had to let her go for the betterment of the entire company. She was making the workplace an uncomfortable place to be. I've told you to do the same thing (in an earlier chapter) if you find you can't fix one of your problem child employees. I would never tell you to do something I would not be willing to do myself. Such is the case with this story.

Here's part of the email message she sent me several months after we released her:

As far as a mentor, Dave, you are the only person in my life that has taken the time to guide me into being a better person. I understand I worked for you and you did this with all your employees, but you did not have to. Like I said, everything happens for a reason. I am still honored to say I was one of your employees.

Remember the chest you were given for Christmas with all the notes/letters from each employee telling you what you mean to each of us? I remember what I had written and I still feel the same way. I thank you for all you do. With that being said, I would still like you to be my mentor (even though I am no longer working for you).

By the way, I never really used to read books. Now, thanks to you, I read every day. I don't read trash either. Most of the books I read are to help me be a better person, inspiring, or something business-related. If you have any suggestions on great books, please let me know.

The article you sent me says, "pick an idol and 'act as if.'" Well Dave, you are that "idol" for me. I could write a book on what you have taught me. I know I only worked for you for 3.5 years, but they were the best 3.5 years of my life."

As you can see, she asked me to be a mentor to her, and I agreed to do that. Even though she no longer works for me, I still care about her deeply, and only want the best for her future.

She's currently reading several books I have suggested to help her become what she is meant to be in life. Though she's made mistakes, I'm proud that she's taking action to turn her life around for the better. Most people wouldn't.

I'll bet you've had a similar situation like this yourself. If you haven't, you probably will in the future.

Sometimes your people will break your heart, and disappoint you. But, in the end, it's worth the pain to be able to see so many others live the lives they wouldn't have ever dreamed of living if not for you. That's rewarding, and it is the best part of being a manager.

William James, the American Philosopher and Psychologist, once wrote:

> *"The greatest use of a life is to spend it*
> *on something that will outlast it."*

Helping people become **better** in everything they do and in everything they are should be the goal of every manager. If you do this, you will be well on your way to creating a legacy for yourself within your entire company. You'll be the manager they'll talk about and put forth as the example of how to do it right long after your career ends. But more importantly, you will find immense satisfaction and pride in making a difference in the lives of those around you, both at work and at home.

NO amount of money can ever buy that.

That, my friend, is TRUE Success!!!

Chapter 10

You have a VERY Important Decision to Make, so... Choose Wisely!

I sincerely hope you have benefitted from reading my book. It's been a labor of love as I have spent many long hours writing it. I can't tell you how many times I went back into each chapter and thought, "I can phrase that better," or, maybe, "I have a better story to illustrate that point!"

Knowing that every author, painter, and sculptor always wishes they could go back and change something in their work, I continuously struggled with what I had written. In my younger days, I used to paint pictures (landscapes mostly) and I always felt that way about every painting I did. I'm a bit of a perfectionist that way. I guess it's an indicator of how much I want this book to help change your life for the better.

Having been blessed to be immensely successful, I genuinely want the same experience for you.

As I've said earlier, I've been poor and I've been wealthy. I know the struggles of each. But, that being said, I would not take away the times when we struggled to have something to eat, and the times I said, "Honey, we can only spend $125 dollars this week on food. Please don't go over that amount. OK?"

Of course, she would, and we'd always have arguments about that.

At times our financial situation was a bit like playing Whack-a-Mole in that we would wait to see who would scream the loudest to get paid that week, and they would receive a small check to shut them up.

I hated the feeling that I wasn't providing the life my wife and children deserved. I know what it feels like to have a family bring presents over to our house for our kids because we didn't have enough money to buy them ourselves. It ripped my heart out of my chest. Truthfully, I briefly thought of suicide once, but could never leave my wife and children alone. Yeah, I'm human too.

Here's the good news: These troublesome times molded me, and I thank God I was fortunate enough to learn valuable lessons from going through each of them.

Notice I didn't say, "I liked them." I'm not completely insane! But, say what you will, they made me a better, and more compassionate man than I would have been otherwise.

I definitely believe this statement as well:

> *How can one appreciate the Mountains...*
> *if they've never been through the Valleys of Life?*
> **I believe that EVERY day is a gift from God to me,**
> **to us. What we do with it is entirely our choice**.

Before I close the book, I need to cover something critically important, so let's talk for a moment about your...

Work-Life Balance.

If you recall, I spoke earlier about thinking long-term on everything you do. That applies doubly here. It doesn't matter if you become the most successful manager in the history of the world IF you destroy your relationships with your family and friends in the process.

One Bible verse our Dad made us memorize as kids was **Mark 8:36**. It goes like this, **"For what shall it profit a man, if he shall gain the whole world, and lose his own soul?"**

If you alienate those in your life, and sacrifice them on the altar of your career ambitions, you'll be a very unhappy person (and all alone) in the latter days of your life.

Knowing that, I ask you to look at your life and make some hard choices as to the best use of your time at work AND at home. If you are one of the misinformed individuals who think that spending an hour a week with your spouse, or with your kids, is enough... it's not. Forget that junk about Quality over Quantity. It's a lie. Invest TIME into your relationships first, and then you can make sure it's quality time. There's no NFL or college football game, or Nascar race, that is more important than your family.

I've never heard of anyone reaching the end of their life and saying, "I wish I could have watched one more basketball game!" That never happens. But, I have heard many folks lamenting the fact that they did not spend enough time with their spouse, children, and grandchildren. In the end, that's all that matters.

Choose Wisely

Did you see the movie, *Indiana Jones and the Last Crusade*? Great movie. Do you remember the part near the end of the story that took place in the cave where Indiana Jones (Harrison Ford's character) met the old knight who had been guarding the Holy Grail for centuries? If you recall, there were dozens of types of drinking cups, or *chalices* (some golden, some jeweled, some rather common and plain).

The evil Nazi leader, who had captured Indy and his father, was deciding which cup to choose to drink from that would convey to the drinker eternal life.

207

Well, as you remember, the guy didn't do such a great job, and he picked a golden cup as his choice. He dipped the golden cup into the holy water pool and drank from it. Bad idea. He immediately began aging years in mere seconds, and died an excruciatingly painful death. The old knight said, "He chose poorly."

You can see this video at www.Top1oManager.com/Resources. Click on the "Choose Wisely Video."

Knowing that his father was about to die from a gunshot wound to the chest, Indy knew he had to act fast! He surveyed the dozens of cups remaining. As he pondered which cup to choose, the old knight cautiously said to him... "Choose wisely."

As you can probably guess, if you haven't seen the movie, our hero chooses wisely, chooses the cup of a common carpenter (the profession of both Jesus and his earthly father, Joseph), dips it into the pool and drinks. Nothing happens. He doesn't die. He immediately dips it into the pool again, and runs to give his father a drink. As you can guess, our hero saves the day.

Now is the part where you have some hard choices to make.

I challenge you to ignore the notion of putting this book up on the shelf (or downloading another book on your iPad or Kindle), and simply forgetting what you've READ here.

Notice I didn't say *Learned*.

If you put this book away without taking action on what you've read, you're "no better than a person," as Mark Twain said, "who cannot read." You will have learned nothing!

Not to preach to you (because that is not my intent), but in the first chapter of the book of John it says rather beautifully: **"But be DOERS of the word, and NOT hearers only, deceiving**

yourselves. For if anyone is a hearer of the word and not a doer, he is like a man observing his face in a mirror; for he observes himself, goes away, and immediately forgets what kind of man he was."

That's where you are right now as you are finishing my book. You can merely take what you read in my book, think "what a cool idea," but do nothing, and then move on to other things.

Yes, you can choose to ignore every thought of "That sounds like something we definitely need to do!" Or, you can choose to go back through each chapter and create a systematic plan to implement the lessons I've taught you. The latter option is the only way to actually change your life and career for the better.

So, what will you do now?

To you I humbly plead... Choose Wisely!

My book has introduced you to concepts and principles you probably did not know. It was not written to merely entertain you. Yes, hopefully, you've laughed as you've read some of my stories, but they were meant to help you LEARN certain principles.

If you simply read them, and nothing has changed in your thinking, then our time together has been wasted. What a tragedy that would be!

Again I say, "Choose Wisely!"

If you recall, I've literally guaranteed your success IF you follow my **Management R.E.W.A.R.D.S. Principles.**

I've told you that I will give you your money back IF your world doesn't radically change when you IMPLEMENT what I've taught you. I challenge you to show me another author who backs up their claims this way!

You have read the book if you've gotten this far, and I congratulate you. You've already done more than the average American will do all year. But, merely reading it won't change your life. That can only happen when you take action on implementing what I've shared with you. Anything less is a waste of time.

I can't wait for you to experience the thrill your team members will have from reading a book together as a team, and sharing the ideas of what they got from that chapter. I assure you, it will only make you wish you could go back in time and start this team building process much earlier in your career. Just like I would, if I could.

I can't wait to hear your story of how your own Book Club meetings changed your employees' lives to the place where they tell you, like mine have told me: "That book changed my life, Dave, and saved my marriage!" Or maybe you'll hear, "That book helped me learn how to manage my money better, and as a result we'll be out of debt this year!"

As exciting as that is to imagine, it doesn't come close to experiencing it first-hand. You'll never understand what I mean unless you take action TODAY.

Not tomorrow. TODAY!

It won't be easy, but it WILL be worth it in the end. I assure you.

"The few who DO are the envy of the many who only watch."
—Jim Rohn

One more short story before we go:

A young girl, about the age of six, and her father were taking a walk along a mountain path, and something just off the path caught the young girl's eye. It was a low-hanging branch with a small cocoon attached. As they say, "Timing is everything." They were there to see the butterfly struggling to escape the confines of its cocoon.

As they watched this amazing event that few have seen, the young girl became impatient, and said, "Daddy, let's help him. He can't get out! Let's open the cocoon a little bit to help him." Just as she reached out to help the butterfly escape the cocoon, her father reached out, grabbed her hand and gently pulled it back.

He whispered, "Let's just wait a little longer and see how he does."

The father knew that if they helped the butterfly escape the confines of the cocoon without it first struggling and squeezing through the small opening (which would push all the water from its newly formed wings)... they would kill it. He knew, with that much fluid still in its wings, it would never be able to fly.

Finally, though you know it seemed like forever to the little girl, the butterfly emerged completely, stood on the edge of the cocoon for a few seconds, flapped its beautifully colored wings, and silently flew away.

Though it seems like such an insignificant thing to you and me, it most certainly isn't to the butterfly. It's off on a whole new adventure, having always crawled everywhere it went before entering the cocoon.

Just as the father and the little girl witnessed the butterfly take flight and fly away, I want you to experience that same thrill when you see an employee that you've personally hired, groomed, and mentored... leave your cocoon (your business) to become the leader of their own business or department. I've been fortunate to experience this metamorphosis of my people over and over again in my career! It's extremely rewarding. In fact, I just got an email from one former member of my team today, telling me the things I taught her have changed her life.

Messages like the ones from past employees, current employees, friends and family members, who I have been able to touch in some way through the years, mean a great deal to me.

Several years ago, I started keeping these in a 12x18 wooden chest on my dresser, and I have so many cards, letters, and printed emails in there now that the lid won't shut completely. It's safe to say that if there's ever a fire in my house, I will grab the family photos first, and my "treasure chest" second. Hmmm.... maybe I should add my wife, Janet, in there somewhere. Ha!

If you were to look at the calendar of my life, as I am now 56 years of age, you would assume my management career is winding down.

You would be wrong.

I love what I do, and I only want to build bigger and better things in the future. And, I want that same feeling and success for you.

Management is fun. Well, it's fun if you have the right people surrounding you every day. If you don't... well, it can be a mental hell.

Yes, I know it has its good days and bad. It's like anything else in that regard. But the truly wonderful thing about leading others, truly leading them, is that you get to help change their lives for the better. And, better still... you have a front row seat to watch their metamorphosis from their caterpillar stage into the beautiful butterfly you knew they could become. Few people in life will be fortunate enough to have this opportunity. Please don't think that's a trivial thing. It isn't.

Now you have a decision to make. I repeat the same warning given to Indiana Jones... "Choose wisely" and continue to work toward becoming the "Top 10 Manager" you were meant to be!

And finally...

Many times readers have questions on how to implement a particular principle I've shared. If you are one of those readers: Ask away!

I'd love to hear from you. I'd love to have you share with me the things you've learned, and more importantly, how you implemented them during your career. I want to hear the stories (in addition to yours) of the lives of employees and family members that have been changed from your efforts. Yes, I want your story. I may even do a follow-up book featuring the best stories I receive.

Note: With your permission, I may also put them on our website, at www.Top10Manager.com/Resources, for others to learn from your success. Please look for the "Submit My Story" link, and submit your stories there. Thanks. Remember, we're more successful as individuals when we share our victories and mistakes with each other.

If you feel I should have covered a particular aspect of management, or didn't clarify something as well as I should have, please let me know that too.

Please send your questions, ideas, stories, and/or suggestions to: davidlong@top10manager.com

And, if you would, please, I would really appreciate it if you would write a short review on Amazon once you've completed the book and seen the value of what I'm sharing with you. Thank you, in advance, for doing that for me.

Always seek to learn something new each day, and then share what you learn with others. You will never truly master anything unless you teach what you know to someone else. That philosophy has served me well, and I know it will do the same for you. Please, if you've benefitted from my book, share it with anyone you know could benefit from reading it.

Thank you, again, for investing some time with me. I truly appreciate it and YOU! I consider you my newest friend. If you're ever in my area (Wilmington, North Carolina), please let me know you're coming, because I'd love to take you to lunch! It would be my honor and privilege.

Build yourself.
Build your team.
And, together, you will be...
Built to Lead.

Sincerely, your biggest fan, and someone who truly cares about your success!

David Long

Your "To Do" List for Becoming a Top 10% Manager

1   Lead Your People. Do not manage them. Being the Leader you should be pulls people toward your goals and the goals of the company. Being merely a "manager" forces you to use a cattle-prod to get the results you want, and builds no loyalty between you and your people. You'll lose many great employees if there is no loyalty to you.

2   Build Relationships with Your People. Forget this, "No Fraternizing with the Troops" junk! Napoleon didn't manage his troops; he led them, and they were willing to die for him. How loyal are your people to you? Work on improving that loyalty every day – with every employee!

3   Leaders are Learners. If you don't read and try to improve constantly, your people won't. If you read and share what you're learning, then others will follow suit. You'll have a much stronger and more bonded management team when you're all committed to improving yourselves and your people. Turn off the idiot box (TV) and read 30 minutes a day to start, but try to build up to at least an hour a day. I read 3+ hours everyday, and it's made me millions.

4   Get the Right People on Your Team – NOW! Remember, if you have a weak team, your career will not be successful. Hire, train, prune, and promote your best people. This is the number one aspect upper management wants from you. Having the right people on your team shows others that you are a true leader capable of higher positions.

5   Start Your Book Club Meetings Immediately! Grow your people as you grow yourself. There is nothing that I have developed

that comes anywhere near the results we have received from the times we are together as a team discussing topics that make us better team members, leaders, parents, neighbors, and friends.

6   Start Your Mastermind Group TODAY! I shared with you all the reasons to have your own Mastermind Group, so be the first of your company's leaders to start your own group. Call the prospective members, and share with them the resources I've shared with you. If you wait, someone else will call you! Your chance to be seen as a true leader will pass to someone who took action. Thinking about doing something means nothing. Taking Action is all that matters!

7   Identify and Spend Time with Your Winners. During your Book Club meetings you'll see employees stepping forward, and emerging from their shells. Encourage, but don't force this to happen. When you see talent and a potential leader in the group, encourage that person to pursue a leadership position, and show them this book, *Built to Lead*. It will shorten their ramp-up time and learning curve to become someone you can promote.

8   Always Keep a Positive Attitude! Thomas Jefferson's advice about Attitude bears repeating here: "Nothing can stop the man with the right mental attitude from achieving his goal; nothing on earth can help the man with the wrong mental attitude." Your attitude is the foundation from which your employees will base and form theirs, so make yours the best in the company! Others will notice, I assure you. Never bad-mouth the leaders above you; your people will do the same to you, and rightly so. Don't teach them bad habits. Display the attitude you would want your people to emulate.

9   Persistence is the Key to Success. Keep doing the right things, day in and day out, and it WILL pay off for you. Don't take the path of least resistance. ALWAYS think long-term with every decision you make. If you think short-term too many times, your career will be short-term as well. You're better than that!

10   Recognize Your Winners! Remember, "What gets Recognized... gets Repeated!" If you want more employees to be loyal to you, be loyal to them first by recognizing their accomplishments. Everyone wants significance. Give it to them, or you'll lose them to someone who will. William James once said, "The Deepest Principle of Human Nature is the Craving to be Appreciated!" If you fail to realize and use this to your advantage as a leader, you won't be one very long! Go to www.MyEmployees.com and you'll find help to do this.

11   Develop Your Own Mentorship Program. If you recall from an earlier chapter, I shared with you my "Shark's Teeth Leadership Development Program." Create your own, so that when there's a vacancy on your team, you aren't scrambling around trying to get someone to fill the spot who may not be qualified. Remember, have your leaders developed to the level where you have a surplus of "teeth" ready to pop into the available leadership spots on your team or other teams. Either way, you're the leader who trained them, and that's the quickest path to upper management in your company!

12   Success comes from developing and helping others. Success does not mean "more money." Once you have it, as many have found out, you'll see what I mean. Bigger and more expensive things do not bring happiness. Growing yourself and those around you does. That includes your family and friends as well. "Teach a man to fish, and you feed him for a lifetime!" That's our goal. Find and develop leaders from all who cross paths with you in life.

Read, and endeavor to live by my "R.E.W.A.R.D.S. Principles" EVERY Day... and you'll soon know what true success really is!

God bless!
David Long

You have a VERY Important Decision to Make, so... Choose Wisely!